Nigeria
and the Challenge of
Federalism

Nigeria
and the Challenge of
Federalism

Ike Okonta

Daraja Press

Published by
Daraja Press
https://darajapress.com

ISBN:9781990263392

Cover design: Kate McDonnell

This writing of this book was made possible through a grant to the
author from the West Africa office of the Ford Foundation. The opin-
ions expressed herein do not necessarily reflect the position of the
Foundation.

Library and Archives Canada Cataloguing in Publication
Title: Nigeria and the challenge of federalism / Ike Okonta.
Names: Okonta, Ike, 1963- author.
Identifiers: Canadiana (print) 2022016147X | Canadiana (ebook)
    20220161518 | ISBN 9781990263392 (softcover) | ISBN
    9781990263408 (PDF)
Subjects: LCSH: Federal government—Nigeria. | LCSH: Nigeria—Poli-
    tics and government.
Classification: LCC JQ3090 .O36 2022 | DDC 320.9669—dc23

TABLE OF CONTENTS

No Nigerian arrangement is permanent unless that which has been reached by negotiated compromise.

Peter Enahoro: *How To Be A Nigerian*

1

Nigeria's Flawed Federalism:
The Colonial Roots

Abdulsalaam Abubakar, a retired general and former Head of State who inaugurated Nigeria's Fourth Republic in May 1999 when he handed over power to President Olusegun Obasanjo, was in a sober and reflective mood on the evening of 30 September 2020. The occasion was an interview with Channels, a Lagos-based television network, to mark the country's 60th Independence anniversary. Declared General Abubakar: 'Nigeria is being pulled apart in several directions. Arewa Consultative Forum is making demands for the North. Afenifere is clamouring for Yoruba interests, and Indigenous People of Biafra wants the defunct Biafra to be resurrected. Today, the country is more divided than at any previous time in its history.[1]

Nigeria, Africa's most populous country and the continent's largest economy, is in trouble. The 23 November 2020 editorial of Punch, a leading newspaper, illustrated this fact in graphic terms:

> The government has lost control of parts of the country to bandits and terrorist insurgents. It is arguably the only country not at war where soldiers are keeping the peace in 33 out of its 36 states. Figures by Amnesty International that 1126 persons were killed, and 380 others abducted by bandits from January to June are regarded as understated. Even the governors cannot travel safely on the highways in many northern states. Insurgents and bandits ambush, kill and abduct police officers and soldiers. Apart from hosting three of the world's five most deadly terrorist groups – Boko Haram, ISWAP and Fulani militants – insecurity, in the form of kidnapping, armed robbery, cult and gang violence, piracy, rape and drug abuse, has created food insecurity and 2.5 million refugees, over

---

1 General Abdulsalaam Abubakar, interview with 'Newsnight', *Channels Television*, 30 September 2020.

200,000 of whom are taking refuge in neighbouring countries.[2]

Ironically, fate had offered General Abubakar an opportunity to launch Nigeria's Fourth Republic on a solid pedestal when he assumed power following the death of maximum dictator General Sani Abacha in June 1998. However, pro-democracy groups were still up in arms following the annulment of the 12 June 1993 presidential election results by Abacha's predecessor in office, General Ibrahim Babangida. Not only were these groups insisting that the presumed winner of the election, Moshood Abiola, be freed from detention and given his mandate, they were also calling for a 'Sovereign National Conference' that would re-examine the country's constitutional problems and listen to the growing clamour of the various ethnic and interest groups for a constitution that would reflect Nigeria's complex diversities.

But General Abubakar chose to do neither. While he dallied, Moshood Abiola died in detention. The demand of the pro-democracy groups for a new constitution was brushed aside, and elections were held in February 1999. Abubakar and his henchmen hurriedly cobbled together in secret a constitution to suit their partisan interests. Finally, they unveiled it for Nigerians when President Obasanjo was sworn into office in May 1999.

The central argument of this book is that the reluctance or inability of Nigeria's political leaders, from colonial times to the present, to craft a federal constitution that will adequately reflect Nigeria's many diversities while at the same time holding the country together as one united entity, is at the heart of the country's current political and socio-economic problems. As the historian Basil Davidson has argued regarding the continent,

> Africa's crisis of society derives from many upsets and conflicts, but the root of the problem is different from these: different and more difficult to analyse. The more one ponders this matter, the more clearly it is seen to arise from the social and political institutions within which decolonised Africans

---

[2] *Punch*, 'Buhari: Nigeria Should Be Re-negotiated,' Editorial, 23 November, 2020.

have lived and tried to survive. Primarily, this is a crisis of institutions.[3]

Similarly, I argue that the Nigerian crisis is a crisis of institutions, the chief institution being federalism.

Theorising Federalism

Kenneth Wheare has defined federalism as 'the method of dividing powers, so that general and regional governments are each, within a sphere, co-ordinate and independent.'[4] Obafemi Awolowo, perhaps Nigeria's staunchest champion of federalism based on the linguistic principle, is even more explicit:

> The only thing which distinguishes a unitary from a federal constitution is where the supreme legislative authority in the state resides. As we have noted earlier on, in the case of a unitary constitution, the supreme legislative authority in the state is vested in one government. Whereas in the case of a federal constitution, the supreme legislative authority is shared between the general or central government and the regional, provincial, or state governments, all of which are coordinated with and independent of one another regarding the powers and functions expressly or by necessary implication vested in them by the constitution.[5]

The concept of federalism is related to such other concepts as quasi-federalism, cooperative federalism, organic federalism, dual federalism, confederation, and decentralisation, which are all terms used to designate shades or levels of federalism. Some conditions have been advanced to account for successful federal government. Two critical ingredients that must be present in a political formation before federalism can be successfully practised are liberal democracy and effective political leadership. Kenneth Wheare is the leading theorist of liberal democracy as the fundamental platform on which the successful practice of federalism rests: 'Dictatorship, with its one-party gov-

---

[3] Basil Davidson, *The Black Man's Burden: Africa And The Curse Of The Nation-State*, New York: Random House, 1992:10.

[4] Kenneth C. Wheare, *Federal Government*, New York: Oxford University Press, 1956, p. 87.

[5] Obafemi Awolowo, *Thoughts On Nigerian Constitution*, Ibadan: Oxford University Press, 1966, p. 23.

ernment and its denial of free election, is incompatible with the working of the federal principle. Federalism demands forms of government that have the characteristics usually associated with democracy or free government. There is a wide variety in the forms which such government may take, but the main essentials are free election and a party system, with its guarantee of a responsible opposition.'[6] Scholars like Adele Jinadu have questioned the link between federalism and democracy. Argued Jinadu,

> the debate on whether military rule, one-party rule, etc., are compatible with federalism, becomes irrelevant, for surely, they can be compatible with each other. The question of whether they make for successful federal government or not then becomes a question of empirical investigation. Either way there is no conclusive evidence, that so-called democratic institutions guarantee successful federal government.[7]

Regardless of Adele Jinadu's stance, experience has shown that liberal democracy is pivotal to the successful practice of federal government. The United States is the first federal state in the world. Following the successful prosecution of the anti-colonial war against Great Britain, delegates of the original 13 American colonies assembled in Philadelphia in 1787 and fashioned out a federal constitution, dividing powers between the central government and the various colonies, subsequently called states. Significantly, the colonies had earlier experimented with confederation, but the passage of time had forged economic and social bonds between them, and they found the strictures imposed by this arrangement irksome. They subsequently opted for federalism. The drafting of the federal constitution was preceded by a robust democratic debate, with the result that the document that later emerged was arrived at by consensus. The American federal constitution has endured ever since.

The second vital ingredient necessary for federalism to thrive and prosper is effective political leadership. Federalism is by design a system that depends on consensus, give and take and the ability to take the long view for it to work. Where political leaders adopt oppor-

---

[6] Kenneth C. Wheare, *Federal Government*, p. 47.

[7] L. Adele Jinadu, 'A Note On The Theory Of Federalism,' in A.B. Akinyemi, P.D. Cole, and Walter Ofonogaro, Editors, *Readings On Federalism*. Lagos: Nigerian Institute of International Affairs, 1979, p. 23.

tunism and 'winner takes all' practices as political weapons, the federal government is liable to break down. Chinua Achebe, the novelist, has written about some of Nigeria's First Republic leaders thus:

> In spite of conventional opinion Nigeria has been less than fortunate in its leadership. A basic element of this misfortune is the seminal absence of intellectual rigour in the political thought of our founding fathers – a tendency to pious materialistic wooliness and self-centred pedestrianism. A perceptive student of Nigerian politics, James Booth, has drawn attention to the poverty of thought exhibited in the biographies of Dr Azikiwe and Chief Awolowo in contrast to the expressions of ideology to be found even in the more informal works of Moboya, Nyerere and Nkrumah![8]

In a solemn vow made by Azikiwe in 1937, he pledged: 'that henceforth I shall utilize my earned income to secure my enjoyment of a high standard of living and give a helping hand to the needy.' Obafemi Awolowo was even more forthright about his ambitions:

> 'I was going to make myself formidable intellectually, morally invulnerable, to make all the money that it is possible for a man with my brains and brawn to make in Nigeria. Thoughts such as these are more likely to produce aggressive millionaires than selfless leaders of their people. An absence of objectivity and intellectual rigour at the critical moment of a nation's formation is more than an academic matter. It inclines the fledgling state to disorderly growth and mental deficiency.'[9]

Sir Ahmadu Bello and Alhaji Abubakar Tafawa Balewa also do not escape the charge of mental deficiency as their doings during Nigeria's First Republic show. However, the country's colonial rulers are the chief culprit in the absence of democracy and poor political leadership to birth a malformed federalism in Nigeria. Indeed I argue that the Nigerian crisis has its roots in its colonial beginnings.

---

[8] Quoted in Orock, Rogers. "Chinua Achebe's postcolony: A literary anthropology of postcolonial decadence." *Africa: The Journal of the International African Institute*, vol. 92 no. 1, 2022, p. 71-92. *Project MUSE* muse.jhu.edu/article/846443.

[9] Chinua Achebe, *The Trouble With Nigeria*, Enugu: Fourth Dimension Publishers, 1983, pp 13-14

Colonial Rule and Crisis

Nigeria as a colony of Great Britain began life in 1900 when the British Government took over the administration of the Royal Niger Company's Northern territory and declared it the Protectorate of Northern Nigeria. This new Protectorate was placed under a British High Commissioner. Before this, British traders and proconsuls had been active in Lagos and, further to the west, in Warri, Bonny and Calabar. In 1906 the Colony and Protectorate of Lagos comprising the Colony of Lagos and other parts of Yorubaland were merged with the then Protectorate of Southern Nigeria, which consisted of the former Eastern and Midwestern Regions to form the Colony and Protectorate of Southern Nigeria. This Protectorate was placed under a British Governor.[10] On January 1 1914, the Protectorate of Northern Nigeria and the Colony and Protectorate of Southern Nigeria were amalgamated into one administrative entity and named the Colony and Protectorate of Nigeria. One British Governor was administering the entire country. The two Protectorates of Northern and Southern Nigeria and the Colony of Lagos retained their identities under two Lieutenant-Governors and a Commissioner based at Kaduna, Enugu and Lagos, respectively.

In 1922 a Legislative Council for Nigeria was created. The Legislative Council of Nigeria had the power to make laws for the Colony of Lagos and the Protectorate of Southern Nigeria. In contrast, the Governor alone had the power to make laws for the Protectorate of Northern Nigeria. Of the 52 members of this first Legislative Council of Nigeria, none represented the North. In 1939, the Protectorate of Northern Nigeria was renamed Northern Provinces of Nigeria. The Protectorate of Southern Nigeria was divided into two administrative units, namely the Eastern Provinces of Nigeria and the Western Provinces of Nigeria. In 1945 a new constitution, named after the Governor of Nigeria, Sir Arthur Richards, was introduced. The two objectives of this constitution were 'to promote the unity of Nigeria; to provide adequately within that unity for the diverse elements which make up

---

[10] See Obafemi Awolowo, *Thoughts On Nigerian Constitution* for a summary of constitutional developments in Nigeria from the outset of colonial rule to the end of the First Republic.

the country; and to secure greater participation by Africans in the discussion of their own affairs.'[11]

The Richards Constitution was a novelty in that Nigerians began to participate, albeit indirectly, in their own political affairs for the first time. This constitution, which came into operation in 1946, provided two assemblies in the North: the House of Chiefs and the House of Assembly; it provided for only a House of Assembly in each of the Western and Eastern Provinces. Even so, these houses were deliberative, not legislative. Even worse, Sir Arthur Richards did not consult Nigerians before introducing the constitution, and Nigerian leaders criticised him severely. Following this rejection, preparations were made by the British rulers to introduce a new constitution. Sir John Macpherson avoided Richards' mistake and undertook a nationwide consultation preparatory to crafting a replacement.

Macpherson asked Nigerians questions at the Native Authority (Local Government), provincial, regional and general (all-Nigeria) conferences. Two of the questions are significant for the theme of this book:

- Do we wish to see a fully centralized system with all legislative and executive power concentrated at the Centre or do we wish to develop a federal system under which each different region of the country would exercise a measure of internal autonomy?
- If we favour a federal system should we retain the existing regions with some modifications of existing regional boundaries or should we form regions on some new basis such as the many linguistic groups which exist in Nigeria?[12]

The Northern Regional Conference opted for a federal system of government for Nigeria. The North called for a central legislature In addition to regional legislatures with powers to legislate on several specific subjects. The Eastern Regional Conference also recommended a federal system. Finally, the Western Regional Conference said there should be a federal system in which the constituent states would be formed on an ethnic and/or linguistic basis. The recommendations of the Lagos Colony Conference were similar to those of the Western Regional Conference.

---

[11] Quoted in Obafemi Awolowo, *op cit*, pp 4-5.

[12] Obafemi Awolowo, *op cit*, pp. 6-7.

The General Conference met in Ibadan in January 1950. It recommended to the Secretary of State for the Colonies a form of federal instead of a fully centralized system with all legislative and executive power concentrated at the centre. It also recommended a House of Representatives for the whole country and that each Region should have its own legislature. The Secretary of State for the Colonies accepted some of the recommendations. However, the Macpherson Constitution that came into force in 1951 was not a federal constitution. The Federation that existed under the Macpherson Constitution did not allow the three regions to exercise their powers fully. It was too tight and came to light in 1953 when the issue of Independence for Nigeria was tabled in the central legislature. The North refused to back the motion saying it was not yet ready for Independence. That generated a lot of acrimony nationwide, leading to the breakdown of the Macpherson Constitution in March 1953.

There was another constitutional conference in 1953-54. This conference put Nigeria firmly on the pedestal of federalism. The resulting constitution made provisions for the regional governments to coordinate with and be independent of the Federal Government in their functions. It also regionalized the Public Service, the Judiciary and the Commodity Marketing Boards. The Independence Conference of 1957-58 entrenched fundamental human rights in the constitution and made provisions for the future creation of additional regions and establishing a Judicial Service Commission. The 1963 Republican Constitution abolished the Judicial Service Commission and appeals to the Privy Council.

In summary, Nigeria's constitutional journey from the inception of colonial rule to Independence in October 1960. It must, however, be pointed out that the federalism that the British left behind was placed on a faulty pedestal. Indeed, one of the leading politicians of the First Republic described the British-imposed federal structure as 'an abominable, disrupting and divisive British heritage.' Frederick Lugard, first governor of the Northern Region, adopted the 'Indirect Rule' system wherein the region was governed through the emirs and district heads. Mahmood Mamdani has written of this political innovation thus:

> The functionary of the local state apparatus was everywhere called the chief. One should not be misled by the nomencla-

ture into thinking of this as a holdover from the pre-colonial era. Not only did the chief have the right to pass rules (bylaws) governing persons under his domain, he also executed all laws and was the administrator in "his" area, in which he settled all disputes. The authority of the chief thus fused in a single person all moments of power: judicial, legislative, executive and administrative. This authority was like clenched fist.[13]

Lugard so strengthened the powers of the Northern emir that he became a virtual dictator towering far above the ordinary people. He also attempted to extend this decentralized despotism to the Eastern part of the country when he was brought back to Nigeria in 1912 to unify the Northern and Southern protectorates. As we have noted, federalism and political authoritarianism do not mix. When it eventually came the time for Nigeria to become a federal state, the authoritarian strain introduced by Lugard became a formidable obstacle on the path of the process. Second, while it is true that Nigeria is ethnically and religiously diverse, there was a fluid admixture between various social groups. The Igbo, Hausa-Fulani and Yoruba ethnic nations did not exist as we know them today. Colonial rule, through administrative regulations and other political strategies, highlighted and exaggerated differences between the various ethnic groups. The activities of Christian missionaries who translated the Bible into local languages, the attempts by locals to create town unions and other self-help groups, and the efforts of local politicians anxious to demarcate their ethnic constituencies all exacerbated these social differences. They led to the emergence of full-blown ethnic groups in Nigeria. As we will see later, these ethnic groups, with their roots in colonial times, were antagonistic toward each other. They were unable to adopt the consensual politics necessary for federalism to work.

The amalgamation of 1914 by Frederick Lugard was poorly handled. Whereas there was a desire in the South for the country to be administered as a unified entity, British intentions were purely financial. Unlike the South, the Northern Region was not generating enough revenue to pay its way. According to Jide Osuntokun,

---

[13] Mahmood Mamdani, *Citizen And Subject: Contemporary Africa And The Legacy Of Late Colonialism*, Princeton: Princeton University Press, 1996, p. 23.

> Southern Nigeria in 1912, on the eve of amalgamation of the two groups of provinces, had a revenue of two and a quarter millions Pounds Sterling and a surplus of one million Pounds Sterling compared with Northern Nigeria, which had half a million Pounds Sterling of local revenue including a grant-in-aid of seventy thousand Pounds Sterling.[14]

Southern journalists and other members of the intelligentsia were privy to this fact and wrote about it in their newspapers. Naturally, this generated bad blood between the South and the North.

Even worse, Lugard could not decide what he wanted to do with the amalgamation. A.J. Harding, a first-class clerk in Colonial Office in London, commented after reading Lugard's proposals on the legislative and financial arrangements for the amalgamation, that the country that would emerge was impossible to classify:

> It is not a unitary state with local government areas but a central executive and legislature. It is not a federal state with federal executive, legislative and finances, in addition to provincial executive, legislatures and finances. It is not a personal union of separate colonies under the same Governor. It is not a confederation of states. If adopted, his proposal can hardly be a permanent solution.[15]

Anthony Nwabughuogu has also observed that Lugard strongly desired to keep the North in its 'pristine' state, 'uncontaminated' by the South. He had perfected a system of indirect rule in the North, and he thought opening the territory to free interaction immediately with Southerners would corrupt the system. Indeed, Lugard saw the amalgamation as no more than 'the extension into the South of the Northern system of Native Administration.'[16] Thus Lugard's amalgamation, instead of serving as a platform to bring Northerners and Southerners closer together, became a colonial strategy to deepen divisions be-

---

[14] Jide Osuntokun, 'The Historical Background Of Nigerian Federalism,' in A.B. Akinyenmi, P.D. Cole and Walter Ofonagoro, ed., *Readings On Federalism*, Lagos: Nigerian Institute of International Affairs, 1979, p. 93.

[15] Quoted in Anthony I. Nwabughuogu, 'Unitarism Versus Federalism: A British Dilemma, 1914-1954,' in J. Isawa Elaigwu and G.N. Uzoigwe,ed., *Foundations Of Nigerian Federalism 1900-1960*, Abuja: National Council On Intergovernmental Relations, 1996, p. 39.

[16] Anthony I. Nwabughuogu, 'Unitarism Versus Federalism,' p. 41.

tween the two further. This was to have grievous consequences for the cause of federalism in the country.

Lugard and the Northern emirs had worked out an amicable agreement to keep Christian missionaries out of the North. The consequence of this was that Western education, which was denied to the overwhelming majority of Northerners in the first decades of the colonial period, was carried out mainly by the missionaries. It is, however, significant that the emirs and district heads took care to send their sons to the few schools that were built in the North. That was not the case in the South, where the Christian missions competed to build schools, hospitals and other Western social amenities. This was the origin of the gap in educational attainment between the North and the South, a development that was to have far-reaching consequences for the politics of national integration. In their attempt to shield Northern political leaders from their Southern counterparts, Lugard and his British successors did not bring the two together until 1947, when Northerners began to participate in the deliberations of the countrywide legislative council in Lagos. By then, the leaders of the two parts of the country had become set in their ways and could only look at one another with mutual suspicion. It is not surprising that when a federal structure was eventually imposed on the country by the British in 1954, it was an antagonistic federalism that rested on nearly six decades of colonial-induced division and mutual animosity between the three regions. It was a federalism that could not withstand social and political stress as the politics of the First Republic gathered pace in the late 1950s.

Federalism On Trial: The Failed Politics Of The First Republic

Three major political parties, corresponding to the regional division of the country, emerged in the 1940s and early 1950s to work the 1960 federal constitution with which Nigeria's First Republic was inaugurated. The National Council of Nigeria and the Cameroons (NCNC) was established at the insistence of young students who were protesting against specific actions of the colonial government. Herbert Macaulay, the veteran nationalist, was elected President of the new political party while Nnamdi Azikiwe, the fiery journalist and proprietor of the *West African Pilot*, emerged as General Secretary. The Egbe Omo Oduduwa, an ethnic association of the Yoruba people, was established in 1945 by the lawyer Obafemi Awolowo. It metamorphosed into the Action Group in March 1950. The Northern Peoples Congress (NPC) also developed from an ethnic association, the Jamiyyar Mutanen Arewa, in December 1949. The NPC was the brainchild of the educated elite in the North including RAB Dikko, Aminu Kano, Yahaya Gusau and Abubakar Tafawa Balewa.

Of these three political parties, only the NCNC aspired to a nationwide representation – at least initially. The NPC did not bother to hide that it was intent on dominating the politics of the vast Northern Region. Indeed, the NPC's first action as a political party was to demand at the Ibadan Constitutional Conference in January 1950 that the North be given half of the seats in the proposed central legislature or else the North would secede from the Federation. Obafemi Awolowo followed the North's example by threatening in 1953 to pull the Western Region out of the country if Lagos was not given back to the West. Riots also broke out in Kano in May 1953 following Anthony Enahoro's motion in the House of Representatives asking that Nigeria be given Independence in 1956. The Northern delegation opposed the motion and was subjected to much opprobrium by their Southern counterparts and the Lagos press. Furthermore, the Action Group manoeuvred Nnamdi Azikiwe out of a seat in the Lagos constituency, which he had won on the platform of the NCNC, forcing him to 'retreat' to the Eastern Region where he, in turn, ousted Eyo Ita, a minority Efik. That triggered bad blood and much recrimination between the Igbo, who constituted the majority in the region, and politicians from such ethnic minority groups as the Efik, Ibibio, Ijaw and Ogoni.

The regionalization of politics and the politicization of ethnicity was firmly in place as the countdown to independence commenced in the mid-1950s. The three major ethnic groups – Igbo, Hausa-Fulani and Yoruba – were at each others' throats, even after the regionalisation of most public services following the inauguration of full-blown federalism in 1954. There was a lot of inter-regional squabbling over an appropriate formula for revenue allocation. The leading export revenue earner in the country in the 1950s was cocoa, and the Action Group made a strong case for the principle of derivation to be embedded in the constitution. The North produced cotton and groundnuts while the East produced palm oil, but the revenue derived from these commodities was not as princely as cocoa. Consequently, the North made a case for allocation according to population size, while the East emphasized need. Fiscal review commissions were established beginning in 1946 to work out an appropriate structure of federal finance for the country. Just before the introduction of the federal constitution in 1954, Sir Louis Chick was asked to prepare a revenue allocation formula that would ensure that 'the total revenues available to Nigeria are allocated in such a way that the principle of derivation is followed to the fullest degree compatible with meeting the reasonable needs of the Centre and each of the regions.'[17]

While the Chick Commission emphasised the derivation principle, the Jeremy Raisman Commission that followed it in 1959 played down considerably the principle of derivation and instead placed great emphasis on population, which was regarded as the approximate index of fiscal need. It also laid great stress on the basic responsibilities of the regional governments and the need for an even development of the country as a whole. Oil had emerged as an important player at this time. Mining rents and royalties, instead of going back wholly to the region of origin as previously, were now to be shared equally between the region of origin on the one hand and the Federal Government and the other regions on the other hand. The Federal Government retained 20 per cent, and the other regional governments were to get 30 per cent through a 'Distributable Pool Account.'[18] The recommendations of the Raisman Commission formed the basis for the working of federal finance in the country during the first four years of the First Republic. In 1964 the Binn Commission was appointed to review these fiscal arrangements following the creation of the Midwest Region. This Commission recommended that the Distributable Pool Account should receive 35 instead of 30 per cent of general import revenues and revenues from mining rents and royalties and that the revenue funds in the DPA should be distributed among the regions as follows: Northern Region, 42 per cent; Eastern Region, 30 per cent; Western Region, 20 per cent; and the Midwestern Region 8 per cent.

These fiscal reviews were attended by much ethnic bickering and anger among the regional politicians, further threatening the working

[17] Nigeria (Sir Louis Chick), Report of the Fiscal Commission On The Financial Effects Of The Proposed New Constitutional Arrangements, London: HMSO, 1954.

[18] F. Akin Olaloku, 'Nigerian Federal Finances: Issues And Choices,' in A.B. Akinyemi, P.D. Cole, and Walter Ofonagoro, ed., Readings On Federalism.

of the fragile federalism in place in the country. However, two developments, one countrywide and the other in the Northern Region could have prevented the centrifugal drift if they had been allowed to mature and prosper. The first was the emergence of the Zikist Movement in February 1946. Founded by young and fiery nationalists who drew inspiration from the writings of Nnamdi Azikiwe in the *West African Pilot*, the Zikists called for independence by 1950, socialism, and the creation of smaller states in the three regions. Membership of the Movement was drawn from the North and South of the country, and it eschewed the ethnic sentiment plaguing the three major political parties in that period. Nnamdi Azikiwe, afraid of the possible reaction of the colonial government to the Zikist Movement, denounced its members in his column in the West African Pilot. The colonial government subsequently cracked down on the Movement and jailed some of its members, including the fiery and charismatic nationalist, Raji Abdullah.[19]

The second development was the emergence of the Northern Elements Progressive Union (NEPU), founded by the politician Aminu Kano in 1950. NEPU was, unlike the NPC, an ideologically-driven political party. Also, unlike the NPC, which enjoyed a cordial and symbiotic relationship with the British, NEPU made it clear that colonialism was a major cause of misery and poverty in Nigeria and that the time had come for the British to quit the stage. 'All parties,' declared NEPU in its radical manifesto of 1950, 'are but the expression of class interests and as the interest of the Talakawa is diametrically opposed to the interest of all sections of the master class, the party seeking the emancipation of the Talakawa must naturally be hostile to the party of the oppressors.'[20] NEPU was very popular among the Northern peasantry and the working class. The NPC and the British colonialists began to harass its members and ensured that they did not emerge victorious in the polls. Had the departing British allowed NEPU to thrive, it would have balanced out NPC's narrow and divisive politics in the Northern Region and the tragedy that befell the First Republic would have been avoided.

---

[19] For details of the emergence, politics and subsequent crushing of the Zikist Movement, see Mokwugo Okoye, *A Letter To Dr Nnamdi Azikiwe*, Enugu: Fourth Dimension Publishers, 1979.

[20] Basil Davidson, *The Black Man's Burden: Africa and the Curse of the Nation-state*, James Currey, 1992, p. 109.

The last opportunity to place Nigerian federalism on a firm footing before the First Republic began life in October 1960 was the Willink Commission which was set up as a fallout of the 1957/1958 Constitutional Conference to 'enquire into the fears of the ethnic minority groups and ways of allaying them.' When this Commission began seating in 1958, it was inundated with demands to create new states in the three regions. The Calabar Ogoja Rivers Movement (COR) asked to form a state in the East. The United Middle Belt Congress (UMBC), led by Joseph Tarka, a Tiv, made a similar demand in the North. The Midwest State Movement also called for a separate state for the non-Yoruba-speaking ethnic minorities in the Western Region. Significantly, all three major political parties – the NCNC, AG, and NPC refused to have new states created in the regions they controlled while supporting state creation exercises in the other areas. The Willinks Commission, in its report, declined to create new states and instead asked that fundamental human rights be entrenched in the constitution. British officials warned the politicians that if they insisted that new states be created, independence would be delayed. Anxious to take power as soon as possible, Nigeria's politicians caved in with the result that the country was gifted an unwieldy federation at independence, with the Northern Region larger in size than the other two combined.

John Stuart Mill, the political theorist, has written about a healthy and balanced federation: 'There should not be any one state so much more powerful than the rest as to be capable of vying in strength with many of them combined. If there be such a one and only one, it will insist on being master of the joint deliberation.'[21] In Nigeria's First Republic, however, the Northern Region was as great, if not greater, both in population and geographic size, than the three other regions combined. Of the 312 seats in the House of Representatives, 167 were allocated to the North, 70 to the East, 57 to the West, 14 to the Midwest and four to Lagos based on population size. Thus, the North had 22 seats more than the whole of the South. The 1959 general elections, which ushered in the First Republic, clearly demonstrated this lopsidedness. While the Northern Peoples Congress (NPC) did not bother to campaign in the South, it won the majority of the seats in its region, enough to put it in a position to control the Federal Government. The NCNC won the majority of the seats in the East and also had a good

---

[21] John Stuart Mill, *Representative Government*, London: Everyman's Edition, 1956, pp. 367-8

showing in the West. The Action Group was able to win the majority of the seats in the West. Given its numerical superiority, the NPC was able to form the government in the centre in a coalition with the NCNC. Abubakar Tafawa Balewa of the NPC became Prime Minister while Nnamdi Azikiwe of the NCNC became ceremonial President. Obafemi Awolowo of the AG became leader of the Opposition.

The three major political parties drew their strength from the three regions they dominated, making pan-Nigerian politics difficult. Thus the First Republic began life with much acrimony, with each political party seeking to undercut the others in the regions they controlled. There was extreme regionalism, and every region vied with the rest to attract amenities for its people, to the detriment of the other regions. Meanwhile, the AG was enveloped by internal crisis following the party's convention in Jos in 1962. Samuel Ladoke Akintola, premier in Ibadan, wanted the AG to cooperate with the Balewa government in the centre and thus attract political posts and amenities for the Yoruba. He also opposed Awolowo's effort to introduce socialism as the party's core ideology. There was a split between Awolowo and Akintola. Attempts by Awolowo to remove Akintola as premier was resisted by supporters of the latter. Ahmadu Bello, leader of the NPC and Tafawa Balewa, the Prime Minister, had always wanted to crush Awolowo, who they saw as a formidable enemy of the North. The AG crisis gave them this opportunity. Prime Minister Balewa declared a state of emergency in the Western Region, sacked the Executive of the Region, suspended Parliament and appointed an Administrator with dictatorial powers, using the flimsy excuse that there was a breakdown of law and order in that Region.

This was the first fatal nail in the federal coffin. Other problems quickly emerged. Attempts by the Tiv, led by Joseph Tarka and the United Middle Belt Congress, an AG ally, to press for political self-determination in the Northern Region was brutally suppressed by the Premier, Ahmadu Bello, who dispatched Federal troops to the area. The nationwide census exercise in 1963 was greeted with much bad blood, each of the three political parties accusing the others of inflating the numbers for their region. The same inter-ethnic acrimony stymied attempts to establish a steel industry.

Meanwhile, Obafemi Awolowo and his followers were accused of plotting to overthrow the Federal Government. They were tried, found guilty and jailed. With Awolowo out of the way, the NPC and NCNC collaborated to carve the Midwest out of the Western Region. The 1964 general election was the equivalent of a civil war. There was much rigging and molestation of political rivals in the various regions. The NPC and Prime Minister Balewa claimed victory and asked President Azikiwe to invite him to form the government. Azikiwe refused, saying that the NPC had not followed the tenets of the democratic game. Each side manoeuvred to win the Army to its side. Following a settlement, Balewa formed the government.

The regional election in the West in October 1965 was even worse. Akintola wanted to retain power. The rump of the AG was desperate to thwart his ambition. Following the election, which Akintola and his political associates massively rigged, the latter claimed victory. The AG cried foul. There was much killing and burning of property. The West was on fire. However, Prime Minister Balewa, actively supporting Akintola with whom NPC was in alliance and desirous of maintaining him in power, pretended that calm prevailed in the West. He even convened a Commonwealth Conference in Lagos while the Western Region burned.[22] This was the situation when the Army struck in the early morning of 15 January 1966.

Historians have adjudged the failed First Republic guilty of three principal offences: regionalism, debilitating ethnic politics and corruption. This is no doubt true. But the chief culprits are the British colonialists who refused to create a stable federation of equal states and allow the flourishing of pan-Nigerian political parties able and willing to pursue a politics embracing ordinary Nigerians regardless of ethnicity or religion. Instead, the British actively encouraged the emergence of a political leadership, particularly in the North that controlled the federal centre, which was extremely parochial in vision and was willing to deploy authoritarian strategies to achieve its ends. As earlier noted, federalism thrives on democracy and good political leadership. These were singularly absent in the First Republic. Thus, the house the British built quickly collapsed when it was tested by the cut and thrust of politics.

---

[22] Eghosa Osaghae offers a detailed account of the collapse of Nigeria's First Republic. See Eghosa E. Osaghae, *Nigeria Since Independence: Crippled Giant*, London:Hurst And Company, 1998.

2
Killing Federalism:
The Soldiers Step In

Two immediate political developments prepared the ground for the military's intervention in Nigerian politics in January 1966. The first was the Tiv uprising in 1963-1964. Obafemi Awolowo and the Action Group adopted the strategy of trying to win over the ethnic minorities in the Northern and Eastern regions to eventually form the government at the centre. Ahmadu Bello, the Northern People's Congress leader, did not like this. So he adopted the counter-strategy of repressing Joseph Tarka and other United Middle Belt Congress leaders who were in alliance with Awolowo. But Bello did not stop here. He got Brigadier Samuel Ademulegun, commander of the First Brigade of the Nigerian Army based in Kaduna where he was Premier, to send troops to the Tiv Division to quell the political uprising there without clearance from the Army Headquarters in Lagos. The Commanding Officer of the 5th Battalion, Lt. Colonel Unegbe, whose troops were to be sent, opposed the move and insisted on proper procedure. However, Unegbe not only failed to stop the troop deployment but was immediately relieved of his command and posted to Lagos on the orders of Ahmadu Bello.[23] Thus, the Tiv crisis was the beginning of the unravelling of proper procedures in the Nigerian Army.

A second development served further to destroy command and control in the army: the Western Region crisis of 1965. The young officers who were despatched to Ibadan and other towns in Western Nigeria were disgusted with Samuel Akintola's politics of brigandage and resented the fact that Prime Minister Tafawa Balewa had given them instructions to bolster Akintola's hold on power. Some of these officers made known their displeasure, which percolated through the Army's rank and file. It was thus only a matter of time before elements of the Army openly revolted against constituted civilian authority. They were no longer practising democracy but using the in-

---

[23] See Alexander A. Madiebo, *The Nigerian Revolution And The Biafran War*, Enugu: Fourth Dimension Publishers, 1980, for a detailed account of the politicisaton of the army during the First Republic.

struments of office to oppress their political opponents. Thus, on the morning of 15 January 1966, the coup makers, led by five young majors – Major Kaduna Chukwuma Nzeogwu, Major Emmanuel Ifeajuna, Major Donatus Okafor, Major A. Ademoyega and Major C.I. Anuforo – struck. In the words of Eghosa Osaghae, 'the violent elections of 1964-65 provided the immediate grounds for the intervention by the young, idealistic officers who wanted to "stamp out tribalism, nepotism, and regionalism" and fight the enemies of progress – the ten percenters, homosexuals, feudal lords and so on.'[24]

But bad planning, sabotage and lapses in execution made the bloody coup only partly successful in the Northern Region where Major Nzeogwu was in charge. Ahmadu Bello, Premier of the North, Samuel Akintola, Premier of the West, and Tafawa Balewa, the Prime Minister, were killed. Several army officers of Northern and Western origin were also killed. Only one senior Igbo officer was killed. The Igbo premiers of the East and Midwest escaped unhurt. This unevenness of killings later provided Northern officers with a potent weapon when they eventually moved against their Eastern counterparts in a revenge coup in July 1966.

Aguiyi-Ironsi: In the Horns of a Dilemma

General Johnson Aguiyi-Ironsi, an ethnic Igbo and general officer commanding the Nigerian Army, had escaped the bloodletting of 15 January. As the dust settled, he got the federal cabinet to hand over the reins of power. In his inaugural broadcast to the country on 16 January, General Ironsi claimed that the transfer of power had been 'voluntary' and that 'the military Government of the Republic of Nigeria wishes to state that it has taken over the interim administration of the Republic of Nigeria following the invitation of the Council of Ministers of the last Government for the army to do so.'[25] General Ironsi made it clear that 'regionalism' was the chief problem with the country. As a first step, he issued Decree 33 banning eighty-one political parties and interest groups and twenty-six tribal and cultural organi-

---

[24] Eghosa E. Osaghae, *Nigeria Since Independence: Crippled Giant*, London:Hurst And Company, 1998. p. 56.

[25] *Ibid*. p. 57.

sations and instituted commissions of inquiry into major parastatals – the Electricity Corporation of Nigeria, Nigeria Railway Corporation, Nigerian Ports Authority and the 'corrupt' Lagos City Council. He appointed military governors for the regions – Lt. Col. Hassan Katsina for the North, Lt. Col. Emeka Odumegwu-Ojukwu for the East, Lt. Col. David Ejoor for the Midwest and Lt. Col. Adekunle Fajuyi for the West.

Military rule, by its very nature, does not favour the practice of federalism for the simple reason that the unified command of the Army has not been trained for such a system of government. General Ironsi did not hide that he preferred a unitary system of government. In another speech on 28 January, Ironsi declared that all Nigerians wanted an end to regionalism and tribal loyalties. He promised that in the public service, efficiency and merit would be the criteria for advancement and that the universities would be re-orientated to serve the genuine interests of the Nigerian populace. Immediately after this speech, Lt. Col. Ejoor, Military Governor of Midwestern State, stated that the new National Government set up by the Army 'was the prelude to the re-introduction of a unitary form of government.'[26] Shortly afterwards, General Ironsi asked Francis Nwokedi, a senior government official, to consider and report to the Supreme Military Council on establishing the administrative machinery for a united Nigeria and the unification of the Public and Judicial Services. This culminated in the passing of the 'Constitution (Suspension and Modification) (No. 34) Decree of 1966' which re-christened the Federal Military Government the 'National Military Government' and re-designated the regions as 'Group of Provinces.' Section 3 of the same decree unified the Federal and Regional civil Services as a single Public Service known as the 'National Public Service.'

There is no doubt that most Nigerians at the time were disgusted with the politics of regionalism and nepotism practised by the politicians of the defunct First Republic. That, however, did not mean that they preferred the unitary government Ironsi had imposed on the country without consulting the public. The Daily Times, the leading newspaper at the time, sounded a note of warning:

> There seems to be misconception among some people that because of the myriad weakness of the last constitution, and be-

---

[26] D.A. Ijalaye, 'The Civil War And Nigerian Federalism', in A.B. Akinyemi, P.D. Cole and Walter Ofonogaro, eds., *Readings On Federalism*, p. 145.

cause of the universal impatience with its shortcomings, we can now take it for granted that Nigerians have picked a unitary form of government for the Second Republic. May be. But only may be... Are we really satisfied that Nigerians necessarily want this?[27]

Ironsi was caught in the horns of a dilemma. Northern officers and political leaders demanded that Major Nzeogwu and the other January 1966 coup plotters be put on trial for killing their senior officers. On the other hand, students and teachers in the Institute of Administration at Ahmadu Bello University, instigated by broadcasts from the BBC, went around Northern towns and cities mobilising public opinion to the effect that the January coup was one-sided, designed to bring the entire country under the domination of the Igbo. Ironsi, they charged, was part of this ethnic scheme.

However, in the South, the coup plotters were hailed as heroes, and the demand was rife that they be released from detention. Ironsi's unification of the public services only worsened matters in the North. The North was at an educational disadvantage compared with the South, and Northern leaders feared that the unification of the public services would see Southern civil servants coming to the North to take over the jobs of Northerners. Northern emirs reached out to General Ironsi and asked that the Unification Decree be re-considered. A few days later, bloody riots broke out in the North. Igbo people and other Easterners resident in the North were killed and their properties destroyed. Some returned to the East. Following intervention by Lt. Col. Ojukwu, Military Governor of the East, Igbos returned to the North as calm was restored.

On 29 July, Northern army officers led by Major Murtala Muhammed and Captain Yakubu Danjuma carried out their revenge coup, murdered General Ironsi and the military governor of Western Region, Lt. Col. Adekunle Fajuyi, and fanned out to the Northern and Western military barracks killing all the Igbo officers and men they laid hands on. The coup plotters had no clear-cut plan to take over the government other than the revenge killings. Indeed, their code word was 'Araba' (secession), and they planned to pull the Northern Region out of the country. These Northern officers had even commenced the

---

[27] *Daily Times*, Lagos, 17 February, 1966.

repatriation of their families from the South to the North.[28] Discipline had broken down. Attempts by Brigadier Ogundipe, a Yoruba and second-in-command to General Ironsi, to take over power was resisted by Northern officers in Lagos who were now in open mutiny. For three days, Nigeria drifted. Nobody was in control. It took the intervention of the British High Commissioner, Francis Cumming-Bruce and the American Ambassador, Elbert Mathews, for a measure of calm to return. Finally, on 1 August, after high-wired manoeuvring, Lt. Col. Yakubu Gowon, a Northerner, took over as Head of State and Commander In Chief of the Armed Forces.

Civil War, Or The Continuation of Politics With Bullets

It could be argued that the civil war which engulfed the country in 1967 was the result of the inability of the military actors, principally Lt. Col. Gowon and Lt. Col. Emeka Odumegwu-Ojukwu, to work out an amicable solution to the challenge of federalism with which they were confronted, following the murder of General Ironsi in July 1966. As Lt. Col. Ojukwu stated as the Army degenerated into factions following the counter-coup of July 1966,

> May I respectfully submit that the Army problem, no matter what we like to say about it is mixed up very closely with the political problem, the question of Government. It depends really on what form of Government you have, for you to decide what sort of Army should serve that Government. If you do it otherwise, it becomes putting the cart before the horse.[29]

Gowon's government in Lagos was confronted with enormous problems from the outset. The counter-coup had left the Eastern Region untouched, and Lt. Col. Ojukwu remained firmly in the saddle as Military Governor. Ojukwu immediately denounced Lt. Col. Gowon's ascension to power as Head of State as illegal. Ojukwu insisted that General Ironsi's fate be made public, and if he was dead, Brigadier Ogundipe, the next highest-ranking military officer, should take his place. Ojukwu further insisted that he would not take orders from Gowon because Gowon was not his senior in the military hierarchy.

---

[28] Eghosa E. Osaghae, *op cit*, p. 61.

[29] Quoted in Robin Luckham, *The Nigerian Military: A Sociological Analysis Of Authority And Revolt, 1960-1967*, Cambridge: Cambridge University Press, 1971.

Gowon was, however, able to consolidate his position as Head of State in the remaining three regions. In his inaugural speech, he suspended Ironsi's unitary decree. He then released Obafemi Awolowo and his followers from prison and established an ad hoc constitutional conference consisting of civilian representatives of the regions. Gowon asked the conference delegations to rule out either the break-up of the country or a unitary state and reduced their choices to four: a federal system with a strong centre; a federal system with a weak centre; a confederal system; or an entirely new political arrangement peculiar to Nigeria.

What is significant about this ad hoc constitutional as it began its deliberations in early September 1966 was that leaders of the opposition like Obafemi Awolowo, Aminu Kano, Joseph Tarka and Anthony Enahoro played a key role. The ensuing deliberations showed that the country's constituent parts had drifted dangerously apart. Leaders of the ethnic minority groups re-activated the clamour for more states to be created in the four regions. The Eastern and Northern Region delegations leaders demanded a confederation where the central government would function as determined by the regions. The Northern delegation proposed that the chairmanship of the central executive council should rotate among the regions from year to year. They suggested that each region would retain its revenue and contribute equally to finance the central government; each region would be free to secede from the region.[30]

The Western and Lagos delegations proposed a federation based on restructuring the four regions into eighteen states and control of the armed forces by the states. The details of their proposal showed that it was not significantly different from the confederal position of the East and North. Only the Midwest delegation, led by Anthony Enahoro, demanded a federation based on creating more states, with a strong centre committed to correcting the injustices of the past and resolving fundamental conflicts in which no state would be allowed to secede. Eghosa Osaghae, the political scientist, has observed:

> As the only minorities region and representatives at the conference, the Midwest was influenced in its position by the historical experience which continually led minorities in Nigeria

---

[30] Eghosa E. Osaghae, *op cit*, p.62

to favour a strong centre as a guarantee against majority oppression in the regions. Such preferences provided the middle
ground which saved the country from breaking up as the majority groups demanded.[31]

By the time the conference adjourned on 3 October 1966, the Northern
delegation had changed its position and was now in favour of federation and the creation of new states. The East did not budge, arguing
that the time was not right for creating new states and that, moreover,
this was a matter for each region to decide.

The renewed mass killing of the Igbo and other Easterners living
in the Northern Region in September 1966 made Lt. Col. Ojukwu recall
the Eastern delegation from Lagos. Igbo people were hunted down in
Northern towns and cities and massacred. Estimates of the numbers
killed are hard to calculate, but some experts have stated that some
80,000-100,000 Igbo and other Easterners lost their lives during this
bloody pogrom in the North. Added to the killing of Ironsi, an Igbo
and other Igbo military officers by Northern soldiers and officers in
the revenge coup of July 1966, sentiments calling for separation from
Nigeria began to harden in the Eastern Region. At the end of September 1966, Ojukwu concluded that the safety of Easterners living
outside the region could no longer be guaranteed and asked them to
return home. He also requested non-Easterners to leave the region. An
attempt was made to patch up differences between Ojukwu and
Gowon when a 'peace' summit of the Supreme Military Council was
held in Aburi, Ghana, between 4-5 January 1967. The Aburi meeting
agreed on a confederal arrangement for Nigeria, but on arriving in
Lagos, Gowon's senior civil servants advised him to renege on this and
instead opt for a federal structure. Gowon subsequently told the nation that he had not gone to Aburi to 'divide' the country. At the end of
February 1967, Ojukwu broadcasted that if the Aburi Agreements
were not implemented by 31 March, the Eastern Region would unilat-
erally put them into effect.

The Gowon government responded by convening another meeting
of the Supreme Military Council in Benin City, which Ojukwu did not
attend. The resulting Decree No. 8 of 1967 conceded to some portions
of the Aburi Agreement but stipulated that the Supreme Military

---

[31] Eghosa E. Osaghae, *op cit,,* p.62-3

Council would be permitted in a state of emergency to take action with the agreement of only three of the four regional Military Governors. Ojukwu interpreted this as an underhand ploy against the Eastern Region and rejected the decree. Faced with solid opposition, Gowon attempted to revive the ad hoc constitutional conference in April 1967. Obafemi Awolowo, however, resigned from the Western delegation claiming that Northern soldiers in the West constituted an 'army of occupation.' Awolowo then stated that if the Federal Government 'by acts of omission or commission' brought about the secession of the East, then the Western Region would secede too.[32] By this time, it was clear to most observers that the Eastern Region was going to secede. On 27 May, the Eastern Nigeria Consultative Assembly mandated Military Governor Ojukwu to declare a 'free sovereign and independent state by the name and title of the Republic of Biafra' when practicable. Gowon reacted immediately to the impending secession. On the same day, he declared a state of emergency, assumed plenary powers and decreed the division of Nigeria into twelve states. The Eastern Region was divided into three states, two for the ethnic minority groups and one for the majority Igbo. Gowon made a tactical move to divide the East and undercut secession. Even so, Eastern Nigerian seceded from Nigeria on 30 May 1967 and proclaimed itself the Independent Republic of Biafra.[33] The immediate reaction of the Federal Government to the secession of Eastern Nigeria was to consolidate what support it had in the rest of the country. Gowon set up a Federal Executive Council made up principally of civilians from eleven of the twelve new states. Obafemi Awolowo became Vice-Chairman of this council and the Federal Commissioner of Finance. A mollified Awolowo went back on his threat to pull the Western Region out of the Federation if the East 'was allowed to go.'

Civil war broke out between Biafra and the Federal Government of Nigeria on 6 July 1967. The war raged for 30 bloody months, the main theatres of battle being in the Biafran heartland. The Federal Government deployed deliberate starvation as a weapon of war, with ships carrying food being prevented from docking in Biafran ports. Malnutrition-related diseases soon set in in Biafra, particularly

---

[32] Robin Luckam, *The Nigerian Military: A Sociological Analysis of Authority and Revolt 1960–67*, Cambridge University Press; 1974, p. 319.

[33] *West Africa*, 30 June 1967

among children. An estimated three million people died of starvation in Biafra. But for the intervention of such charities as Caritas, Oxfam, and the Red Cross, whose aeroplanes carrying food were able to defy the Federal blockade, the number of Biafran dead would have reached four or five million. The war ended with Biafra's defeat on 12 January 1970.[34] Federalism was on trial during the war. For a time during the conflict, the Midwest maintained an uneasy neutrality for the simple reason that it was a divided minority region: ethnic Igbos were in the majority in the officer corps of its army, while the Edo and Urhobo, also ethnic minorities, were broadly sympathetic to the Federal Government. This neutrality ended when Biafran troops led by Lt. Col. Victor Banjo entered the Midwest in August 1967. The Nigerian government counter-attacked and pushed Banjo and his men out of the Midwest a few weeks later. Biafra's defeat paved the way for the subsequent political and economic marginalisation of the Igbo in postwar Nigeria.

The Nigeria that emerged from the debris of the bloody civil war was 'federal' in name but unitary in practice. The war had strengthened the grip of the Army over the North, on the central government and in Lagos. A demonstration of where power lay was the enactment of the Petroleum Decree No. 51 of 1969, wherein all oil and gas resources in the country were placed under the central government's control. Ironically, this was the handiwork of Gowon's powerful Southern minority top bureaucrats – or Super Permanent Secretaries, as they were called: Allison Ayida, Phillip Asiodu and Ime Ebong. Anxious to protect the interests of the ethnic minorities against the depredations of the majority ethnic groups, these permanent secretaries strengthened the power of the central government to the detriment of a healthy federalism. Another blow against federalism was struck a few months later when I.O. Dina, appointed by the Gowon government to review the revenue allocation formula, turned in his report in February 1969. Significantly, Dina was a close associate of Obafemi Awolowo, the Federal Minister of Finance.

By this time, oil had become the chief contributor to national revenue. Dina's report stated that the most urgent problem facing the country was the significant imbalance in economic development

---

[34] For an insider account of why Biafra lost the war see Alexander A. Madiebo, *The Nigerian Revolution And The Biafran War*, Enugu: Fourth Dimension Publishers, 1980.

among the various states. The Dina Committee strongly recommended the principle of fiscal need of the twelve new state governments. It proposed that only 10 per cent of all oil rents and royalties, instead of the previous 50 per cent established previously, should go to the state of derivation. In contrast, the balance of 90 per cent should go to the Distributable Pool Account, which should be renamed 'States Joint Account' for distribution to the various states. A distinction was also made between onshore and offshore oil. Oil-producing states were to be precluded from any share in offshore royalties (60 per cent was to be retained by the Federal Government, 30 per cent to DPA and 10 per cent to a special contingency account). They were to get 40 per cent less than previously under the principle of derivation from onshore royalties. Although General Gowon formally rejected the report of the Dina Committee, this report was to inform revenue allocation in practice throughout his administration. This was the beginning of the marginalisation and exploitation of the oil-producing communities of the Niger Delta, who constituted the ethnic minorities in the Southern part of the country.

With the civil war over, the country's main challenge was when the military would quit the stage and hand over power to politicians. A few months after the war, Gowon indicated that he would hand over power to civilians within two years. However, in his 1 October 1970 Independence Anniversary broadcast, he amended this to 1976. He issued a nine-point programme for transition to civilian rule, which outlined the major problems to be tackled before the handover would take place: census, a system for revenue allocation, a new constitution, the establishment of genuinely national-based political parties as opposed to regional parties of the First Republic, the creation of states, eradication of corruption, implementation of the 1970-74 National Development Plan, demobilisation of soldiers and elections at state and federal levels. However, Gowon's senior civil servants were reluctant to give up power. Corruption was rife, particularly among the state governors and senior civil servants. The latter began to encourage Gowon to stay on. Allison Ayida, one of his 'Super-Permanent Secretaries,' came out in the open in 1973 and declared that Nigeria no longer had a 'ceremonial army' and that the new constitutional arrangement 'must take into account this new and crucial factor.'[35] In an October 1974 broadcast, Gowon announced that the 1976 handover date to politicians was no longer 'realistic.' In July 1975, a faction of the army led by Lt. Col. Musa Shehu Yar'Adua and Lt. Col. Joseph Garba staged another coup and removed Gowon from power. Brigadier Murtala Mohammed, another Northerner, became Head of State. Brigadier Mohammed led the July 1966 revenge coup whose initial goal was to pull the Northern Region out of the Federation.

Mohammed/Obasanjo: Laying The Groundwork for Centralism

Murtala Mohammed took over a Federal Government that the new revenue allocation structure had strengthened. The Federal Government had 'the sole allocative and distributive authority and gave it a domineering fiscal position.'[36] While the creation of twelve states put into place a more balanced federation, the advent of oil, the subsequent oil boom and the central government's determination to control this largesse turned the state governments into powerless satellites orbiting around a now-all powerful Federal Government. Mohammed reorganised the Federal Military Government into three organs: the Supreme Military Council, which remained the highest legislative and executive body; the Council of States, a new subordinate organ composed of state governors; and the Federal Executive Council. Under Gowon, the state governors were members of the Supreme Military Council, but the new arrangement reduced their powers considerably. Senior bureaucrats were also excluded from these law-making bodies except when invited to attend meetings. The Federal Government took control of the universities and created six new ones bringing the number to twelve. Previously a state matter, primary education was also brought under federal government control. Further, television and radio broadcasting were taken over by the Federal Government while controlling shares in the Daily Times and New Nigerian, the two largest newspapers, were purchased. The Land Use Decree was enacted, nationalising all land in the country where previously ethnic

---

[35] Allison Ayida, cited in Billy Dudley, *An Introduction To Nigerian Government And Politics*, London: Macmillan, 1982, p.90.

[36] Eghosa E. Osaghae, *op cit*, p.73

groups controlled their land. The National Security Organisation (NSO) was established to bolster the central government's ability to watch over the entire country and intimidate critics of the new administration.[37] Thus was the groundwork for political centralism laid in the country.

The Mohammed government then set up panels to probe former military governors and other senior government officials. Eleven of the twelve state governors were found guilty of massive corruption: so too senior civil servants. This resulted in the seizure of ill-gotten assets all over the country. Next, more than 10,000 public officials were compulsorily retired or dismissed from the civil service and other public institutions for corruption and sundry misdemeanours. However, this exercise was poorly handled, and the resulting witch-hunting and score-settling led to erosion of morale in the public service. Further, some officials of the Mohammed administration were themselves accused of corruptly enriching themselves. Obafemi Awolowo, who had resigned as Federal Finance Minister, led calls for the military government to hand over to politicians. Finally, on 1 October 1975, the government announced a four-year transition to a civil rule programme. The five-phase transition programme included the creation of new states, drafting a new constitution, local government re-organisation, lifting the ban on political party activities and elections at state and federal levels which would culminate in the handing over of power to civilians on 1 October 1979.

The Federal Government promulgated the Revenue Allocation Decree in the same year, which further departed from reliance on the derivation principle. Under the new allocation formula, oil mining rents and royalties on offshore production were now to be wholly paid into the Distributable Pool Account (DPA). In addition, only 20 per cent as against the previous 45 per cent of mining rents and royalties on onshore production would now go to the state of production. The new Decree gave a considerable boost to the DPA to the benefit of the non-oil producing states. This led to the demand for the creation of more states. In August 1975, a panel headed by Mr Justice Ayo Irikefe was inaugurated to study and make recommendations on the question of states creation. There were demands for at least thirty-two new states. The Federal Government created seven new states in Feb-

[37] Billy Dudley, *op cit*, p. 103.

ruary 1976, bringing the total to nineteen. Making a case for these new states, the Irikefe Panel argued that the need for even development, bringing the government nearer to the people, minimising minority problems, and a balanced federation made the creation of states necessary. The report marked a final departure from a 'federal system in which states were to have a relatively autonomous role as centres of development to one in which states were peripheries of the centre and functioned as administrative agents and distribution outlets for federal resources.'[38]

On 13 February 1976, General Murtala Mohammed, the Head of State, was assassinated in an abortive coup led by Lt. Col. Bukar Dimka. The core of the officers that organised the coup was mainly from the Middle Belt. It was said that the coup plotters disapproved of General Mohammed's 'communist' leanings, among other reasons. Following his assassination, General Olusegun Obasanjo, chief of staff at Supreme Headquarters, became Head of State. Obasanjo strictly adhered to the political transition timetable and paved the way for the emergence of the Second Republic. One of the significant actions of the Obasanjo government, before it handed over power to the politicians, was the inauguration, in 1977, of the Aboyade Technical Committee. This committee sought to ensure that each government in the federation had sufficient revenue to discharge its constitutional responsibilities. It also aimed to balance the imperatives of population, equality, even development, geographical peculiarities and national interest in allocating revenue among states. In its report, the committee recommended replacing the DPA with a Federation Account. It also urged the following sharing formula: Federal Government – 57 per cent; state governments – 30 per cent; local governments – 10 per cent; and special grants account – 3 per cent. Although these recommendations were eventually rejected by the Constituent Assembly, which the government had established to ratify the new constitution on which the Second Republic would be based, the Aboyade Report guided subsequent revenue allocation efforts in the country.

The military's intervention in Nigerian politics in January 1966 dealt a fatal blow to the cause of federalism in the country. General Ironsi's Unification Decree and the subsequent actions of General Gowon, General Mohammed and General Obasanjo succeeded in re-

---

38 Eghosa E. Osaghae, *op cit* p.86

ducing the states from powerful and autonomous centres of politics and development, serving as a check on the centre to small satellites. The Second Republic, which came into being in October 1979, did little to check this reality.

3
Consolidating Centralism:
The Second Republic and After

Nigeria's Second Republic began life, properly speaking, with the establishment of the Constitution Drafting Committee (CDC) by the military government of General Murtala Mohammed on 4 October 1975. Headed by Rotimi Williams, the famous constitutional lawyer, the CDC consisted of 49 academics and other professionals versed in constitution-making. At the inauguration of the committee, General Mohammed outlined several principles to which his government was committed and which he wished to see reflected in the new constitution: a federal system of government; a free democratic system guaranteeing human rights; and the creation of viable political institutions to ensure maximum political participation and orderly succession to power. To achieve these goals, the constitution-makers were urged to consider embodying the following in the constitution: the formation of genuinely national political parties; an executive presidential system of government in which the president and vice-president were elected and brought into office in a manner that reflected the 'federal character' of the country; an independent judiciary; the institutionalisation of corrective organs like the corrupt practices tribunal and public complaints bureau; and restriction on the number of further states to be created. The CDC's final draft constitution embodied all these principles. [39]

A Constituent Assembly headed by Udo Udoma, a Supreme Court judge, was empanelled to consider, amend and ratify the draft constitution. The Constituent Assembly members were drawn from the various states and local government areas. The assembly was more politically representative and partisan, and consequently, its deliberations were noisy and controversial. Indeed, members saw the assembly as a stepping-stone to forming political parties. Issues that generated heated debate in the assembly included revenue allocation, the establishment of a Federal Sharia Court of Appeal, a rotational presidency,

---

[39] Billy Dudley, *op cit*, p. 129. Professor Dudley served as a member of the Constitution Drafting Committee.

the scope of the executive president's powers, freedom of the press and creation of states. Of these, the most controversial, which brought the assembly's deliberations to a halt, was the issue of Sharia. It took the personal intervention of the Head of State for deliberations to resume. The Sharia issue exposed deep fissures between the Southern and Northern parts of the country, fissures that efforts by various military governments did not succeed in bridging. The Supreme Military Council reviewed the work of the Constituent Assembly, and by Decree 25 of 1978, the 1979 Constitution was enacted. The Federal Electoral Commission (FEDECO) was established to conduct elections. Significantly, the new constitution retained the Land Use Decree of 1978 (now known as an act) and the 1969 Petroleum Decree, which placed these vital resources under the control of the central government, and by so doing, robbed the ethnic minority groups of the Niger Delta of their oil. Stated Section 42 (3) of the 1979 Constitution: 'Notwithstanding the foregoing provisions of this section, the entire property in and control of all minerals, mineral oils and natural gas in, under or upon land in Nigeria or in, under or upon the territorial waters and the Exclusive Economic Zone of Nigeria shall vest in the Government of the Federation and shall be managed in such manner as may be prescribed by the National Assembly.'[40]

On 21 September 1978, the ban on political activities was lifted, and political campaigns commenced. About 56 political parties were formed, of which nineteen applied to FEDECO for registration. However, after much deliberation and controversy, FEDECO registered only five of them: National Party of Nigeria (NPN), Unity Party of Nigeria (UPN), Nigeria Peoples Party (NPP), Great Nigeria Peoples Party (GNPP) and Peoples Redemption Party (PRP). Elections into state and federal legislative and executive seats took place in July 1979. The outcome of the presidential election, which took place in August, proved controversial and was the subject of legal litigation. Shehu Shagari of the NPN was eventually declared the victor and was sworn in as President on 1 October 1979 along with the state governors. This ended thirteen years of military rule. However, the centralisation of power and the weakening of vital aspects of the country's federal system which the soldiers left behind, proved problematic for the civilian

---

[40] Quoted in Ken Saro-Wiwa, *Genocide In Nigeria: The Ogoni Tragedy*, Port Harcourt: Saros International Publishers, 1992, p. 85.

regime and indeed was one of the major sources of tension that led to the fall of the Second World Republic.

An American-style executive presidential system was adopted for the Second Republic to avoid the problems that afflicted the First Republic, leading to its early demise. There was a separation of powers between the executive, legislature and judiciary, and there was an elaborate system of checks and balances. A bi-cameral legislature at the centre (called the National Assembly) and a unicameral chamber in the states were established. For the first time, political parties were given constitutional recognition, and FEDECO registered only parties with national spread as distinct from regional ones. In an attempt to remove fears of political and economic domination by one section of the country, the Federal Character Principle was enshrined in the constitution as part of the 'fundamental objectives and directive principles of state policy.'[41] The Federal Character Principle stipulated that appointments to ministerial and other senior government positions and the composition of the armed forces, public service and other agencies of government would be established in such a manner as to reflect the ethnic and religious diversity of the country. However, because there were more states belonging to ethnic majority groups in the federation, applying the Federal Character Principle merely accentuated minority marginalisation. Further, those in control of executive power at the federal level were able to use this power virtually unchecked, relegating ministers to sinecures. This made nonsense of the Federal Character Principle.

Unlike the First Republic, which violated John Stuart Mill's law of federal stability because of the large size of the Northern Region and the marginalisation of ethnic minority groups in the various regions, the Second Republic had 19 fairly well-balanced states with fewer minority problems. Nevertheless, there were regional tensions and fears of domination because the five registered political parties were virtual reincarnations of the ethno-regional parties of the First Republic. The NPN drew its core membership from the North, like the Northern Peoples Congress in the First Republic. The NPP was mainly Igbo, like the NCNC, while the UPN had a predominantly Yoruba following like the Action Group. The PRP was a replication of NEPU. Only the GNPP was a new political formation, but it was also firmly anchored in the

---

[41]See Chapter Two of Nigeria's 1979 Constitution.

North like NPN and PRP. Although the NPN emerged victorious in the elections of August 1979, it found that it needed a working majority to ensure the passage of executive bills. It consequently allied with the NPP, recreating the NPC/NCNC alliance in the First Republic. However, the NPN-controlled Federal Government soon developed an appetite for authoritarianism, transforming the police into a paramilitary outfit that massacred peasants in Bakalori town in Sokoto state and suppressed student protests. Newspapers of rival state governments were sealed off, and the editors were detained.

The over-centralisation of power and corresponding loss of state autonomy which were the legacies of 13 years of military rule, was still evident in the Second Republic, causing enormous strains in the pillars of federalism. Federal-state relations in the Second Republic was characterised by rivalry, confrontation and conflict. Sometimes state governors from political parties other than the NPN would replicate programmes executed by the latter and would even call on their citizens not to obey the directives of President Shehu Shagari. The 1979 Constitution favoured the centre against the states, which led to pitched battles of supremacy between the two. When President Shagari appointed 'Presidential Liason Officers' (PLO) to serve as his eyes and ears in the various states, non-NPN governors stated that the PLOs would not be welcome in their states. Revenue allocation was another source of conflict. President Shehu Shagari had appointed Dr Pius Okigbo, an eminent economist, as head of a committee to work out a new revenue allocation formula for the country in 1981. The resulting Allocation Bill gave 58.5 per cent of federally collected revenue to the Federal Government, 31.5 per cent to the states and 10 per cent to the local government areas. The oil-producing communities were apportioned only two per cent. Some state governors rejected this recommendation, demanding 40 per cent for the states.

As the 1983 general elections neared, the GNPP split into three factions and the PRP into two. Following the dissolution of the alliance between NPN and NPP, several senior members of the latter who had been appointed to ministerial positions by the NPN Federal Government refused to quit their jobs and virtually joined the NPN. As a result, a 'progressive' forum emerged from the various political parties opposed to the NPN and desirous of getting Obafemi Awolowo, leader of the UPN, elected President. The political campaigns were volatile and sometimes violent, and the NPN used its control of the police, newspapers and radio and television stations to intimidate its rivals. The presidential election took place in August 1983 and was followed by the governorship, senatorial, House of Representatives and state houses of assembly elections.

Contrary to expectations, the NPN emerged victorious in these elections. The 1983 elections were widely rigged by the NPN, which controlled the government at the centre. One outcome of the controversial election results was the demand by Yoruba politicians and other leaders of thought for confederalism. According to them, they could not end Northern rule and domination through a legitimate democratic process. Bisi Onabanjo championed this call, UPN governor of Ogun State, who referred to a 'cabal of native imperialism' through massive election rigging and a paramilitary police force that constituted an army of occupation had effected a conquest of the Southern states.

Buhari and the Politics of Centralised Despotism

It has been written of the Buhari regime: 'The return of the military, following the overthrow of the Second Republic, brought in its wake an era of authoritarianism such as had not previously been known in Nigeria's post-independence history.'[42] Military governments are, without exception, authoritarian and undemocratic and operate within a framework that Ben Nwabueze, the legal scholar, referred to as 'lawless autocracy.' This has obvious implications for the operation of federalism in an ethnically diverse and complex country like Nigeria. When power is concentrated in only one person, federalism that thrives on power dispersal and checks and balances, suffers. Scholars like Eghosa Osaghae have speculated that the General Buhari coup was carried out to restore power to a shadowy Northern group called the Kaduna Mafia.[43] They explain this by pointing to the predominance of Hausa/Fulani and Northern Muslim officers in the regime. This resurrected the demand for confederation even as the regime was settling into office. The major advocates of confederation included retired Yoruba military officers like Brigadier Benjamin Adekunle

---

[42] Eghosa E. Osaghae, *op cit.* p. 163.

[43] *Ibid.* p. 167

and General Alani Akinrinade. General Olusegun Obasanjo also joined the chorus and called for more equitable sharing of power and resources and also criticised the Northern hegemonic policies of the new military regime. General Buhari considered the confederation debate dangerous for 'national stability' and was to ban it in July 1985.

In announcing the December 1983 coup, Brigadier Sani Abacha stated:

> Our economy has been hopelessly mismanaged. We have become a debtor and beggarly nation. There is inadequacy of food at reasonable prices for our people... Health services are in shambles as our hospitals are reduced to mere consulting clinics without drugs, water and equipment.[44]

The regime was desperate to implement a programme of economic recovery; so desperate was it to achieve this one goal that it was prepared to deny Nigerians their fundamental human rights in the process. Shortly after taking power, the regime announced a ten-point programme, chief among which were: maintenance of national unity and stability: charting better and more purposeful sense of direction; prudent management of resources; and economic diversification to reduce reliance on oil. Significantly, General Buhari did not mention the restoration of the country's federal structure, which years of military rule and the centralisation tendencies of the NPN politicians in the Second Republic had bartered. Even worse, he proscribed political parties and banned political activities. A nineteen-member Supreme Military Council was established with omnipotent decision-making powers. A National Council of States composed of the state governors was also put in place through which the activities of the state governors would be strictly monitored.

In terms of fiscal relations, the 1982 Revenue Allocation Act was retained, giving 55 per cent of federally collected revenue to the Federal Government; 32.5 per cent to the states; 10 per cent to local governments; 1.5 per cent to the development of the oil-producing areas and 1 per cent to the ecological fund. Thus was the derivation principle, which in the 1954 federal constitution gave regions from which revenue was generated 50 per cent, jettisoned and instead a derisory

---

[44] Excerpts from radio broadcast announcing the 31 December 1983 military coup by Brigadier Sani Abacha.

1.5 per cent allocated to the oil-producing areas. This unfair arrangement was to engender an explosive political situation in the Niger Delta in the 1990s.

The regime then turned its attention to politicians who had misappropriated public funds during the ill-fated Second Republic. Special Military Tribunals were established in Lagos, Kaduna, Ibadan, Jos and Enugu despite the opposition of the Nigerian Bar Association, which called on its members to boycott these tribunals. Persons found guilty were jailed for twenty-one or twenty-five years, depending on the gravity of the crime. With few exceptions, most of the politicians of the Second Republic were found guilty and sentenced to lengthy jail terms and large sums of money recovered from them. The corruption trials further delegitimised Nigerian politicians and, in the eyes of ordinary citizens, strengthened the soldiers claim to govern.

General Buhari's regime promulgated draconian decrees, which increased political authoritarianism in the 1980s and 1990s. The Constitution (Suspension and Modification) Decree no. 1 of 1984 proscribed all political parties and suspended sections of the 1979 Constitution. Decree no. 13 of 1984 established the supremacy of military decrees. The State Security (Detention of Persons) Decree authorised the Chief of Staff at Supreme Headquarters to detain for up to three months (renewable) without trial anyone deemed a risk to national security. This decree enabled General Buhari and subsequent military dictators in the country to detain critics and political opponents without trial in police and security cells. The Nigerian press was also put on the leash. The Public Officers (Protection Against False Accusation) Decree no. 4 of 1984 authorised the arrest and detention and trial of journalists and the closure of any mass media organisation making any 'false statement' embarrassing to public officials. Under the decree, two journalists of *The Guardian* were convicted and jailed for a year. General Buhari's dictatorial excesses galvanised civil society organisations to oppose his government. Organisations such as the Nigerian Medical Association, Nigerian Labour Congress and the National Association of Nigerian Students challenged the regime's draconian decrees. They called on Nigerians to strike out in defence of their fundamental human rights.

William Graf has summed up the difficulties the Buhari government encountered:

The Buhari regime was neither able to overcome the economic crisis it inherited, nor manage it adequately, thus producing a systemic legitimacy crisis. Practically every sector and elite faction were therefore disaffected. True, Buhari had managed at least to contain the economic crisis but the basic dilemma, which his authoritarianism could not address, at least not without further fragmenting the various elite factions, was how to effect economic change without forfeiting elite and mass backing.[45]

To further compound its problems, the regime was widely perceived in the South as a defender of conservative Northern interests. The Supreme Military Council had a Northern majority, and Northern politicians were given preferential treatment in the corruption trials and punishment of officials of the Second Republic. Retrenchments in the public service also favoured the Northern part of the country, making affected Southerners complain. Indeed, the authoritarian decrees of the regime and its lopsided treatment of Nigerians from particular ethnic groups further galvanised the call for confederation by leading Southerners. General Olusegun Obasanjo, a former Head of State, also publicly criticised the regime's 'Northernisation Policy'.

Divisions soon began to emerge within the regime. Shehu Othman has commented: 'In themselves all these divisive issues undermined the credibility and stability of the regime. More fatally, they intensified the strains within the ruling junta.'[46] By the beginning of 1985, two explicit factions had emerged in the military, one led by General Muhammadu Buhari, the head of state and his second-in-command, Brigadier Tunde Idiagbon and another led by General Ibrahim Babangida, Chief of Army Staff. The Babangida faction began to prepare for its ascension to power by subtly discrediting the draconian policies of General Buhari. The former let it be known that it deplored the harassment of journalists and other members of civil society and that it was not the business of the military government to ride roughshod over society. Babangida sent out feelers to leading public figures and business people such as Moshood Abiola, who was also opposed to

---

[45] William D. Graf, *The Nigerian State*, London: James Currey, 1988, p. 169.

[46] Shehu Othman, 'Nigeria: Power For Profit – Class, Corporatism, And Factionalisation In The Military' in D.B.C. O'Brien, J. Dunn and A Rathbone, eds., *Contemporary West African States*, Cambridge: Cambridge University Press, 1989, p. 138.

Buhari and received positive feedback that the Nigerian populace would widely welcome a change of government. In the afternoon of 27 August 1985, General Ibrahim Babangida launched his palace coup and replaced General Buhari as Head of State.

The General Buhari regime had a short life, but its effects on Nigerian federalism were profound. With Buhari, the Nigerian military removed all pretences that Nigeria was still a federal state, that the autonomy of the federating states was to be respected, and that the autonomous spheres of political action that were put in place by the 1954 federal action were still in place.

Ibrahim Babangida and the Endless Transition

Open debate and free expression are the oxygen with which federalism is nurtured. General Ibrahim Babangida promised these two ingredients at the outset of his regime. Coming as he did after the dark and draconian regimen with which General Buhari fed Nigerians, Babangida was like a veritable breath of fresh air. Adebayo Olukoshi, the Nigerian scholar, wrote about the effect of Babangida's regime on Nigerian society thus:

> At no time in Nigeria's postcolonial history has there been so massive an efflorescence of nonprofessional civil associations dedicated to the pursuit of democracy and the rule of law as in the period since 1986 – following the introduction, by the government of Gen. Ibrahim Babangida, of an International Monetary Fund/World Bank-sponsored Structural Adjustment Programme (SAP). Perhaps the only other period in Nigeria's contemporary history when the country witnessed such a massive expression of the democratic quest, manifested through the formation of a host of associations, was the post-World War II period of anti-colonial struggle for independence.[47]

Four moments in the life of the Babangida regime contributed to free-flowing debate and the possibility that federalism would regain its moorings: the political debate supervised by the government-appoint-

---

[47] Adebayo Olukoshi, 'Associational Life,' in Larry Diamond, Anthony Kirk-Greene and Oyeleye Oyediran, eds, *Transition Without End: Nigerian Politics And Civil Society Under Babangida*, Boulder: Lynne Rienner Publishers, 1997, p. 379.

ed Political Bureau; the debate about whether to accept the IMF loan and its attached conditionalities; the appointment of the Constituent Assembly; and the subsequent making of the 1989 constitution.

The Political Bureau was appointed in January 1986 and consisted mainly of political scientists and chaired by Samuel Cookey. Its remit was to generate and guide debate among Nigerians concerning the country's political future. In his speech inaugurating the Bureau, General Babangida stated:

> This Administration does not conceive the Political Bureau as an agency set up simply to serve the national political debate. The Political Bureau will do much more. In addition to guiding, monitoring, analysing and documenting the national political debate, the Bureau will provide an objective and indepth critique of our past political experience in order to serve as background information for the debate. It will also produce the blueprint of a new political model (or models) for the consideration of the Administration.[48]

The Bureau provided thirty issues that the public could address in their contributions to the debate. It was decided that the basic unit of the discussion would be the local government – this was to guarantee adequate participation by the grassroots population. Individuals, groups, and organisations were invited to send memoranda, contribute newspaper articles, participate in radio and television discussions, and organise seminars and conferences on various debate topics. The expressed views of the populace were later synthesised.

One of the most crucial issues the Bureau considered was an appropriate political structure for the country: federal, confederal or unitary. Members of the Bureau had travelled extensively throughout the country to collate views, which exposed them to the social and geographical diversity of Nigeria. Further, most of them were university teachers and were thus aware of the virtues of a robust federal system with considerable decentralisation of authority. While desirous of national unity, they were nevertheless seized by the necessity for devolution of power. The Political Bureau came down firmly on the side of federalism in its recommendation:

---

[48] See *Report Of The Political Bureau, Lagos*: Federal Government Printer, 1987, p. 226.

> Although we appreciate the expression of the sense of struc-
> tural alienation, and the manifest need to correct the ills of
> certain aspects of the existing system, we do not find any com-
> pelling merit in the case for confederalism or in the case for a
> unitary system of government for Nigeria. In fact, we do not
> see any other accommodating and healthier arrangement for
> Nigeria than the continuation of the system of federalism.[49]

The IMF debate provided an occasion for associational life to burgeon
into life. Various groups, including professionals, students, market
women and even roadside mechanics associations, took advantage of
the opportunity to air their views and mobilise support for their position on the issue of IMF participation in the country's economic re-
construction project. The overwhelming opinion expressed was
against IMF participation. General Babangida accepted this position
but, in doing so, announced his intention to introduce a 'homegrown'
programme of economic reforms that would be no less vigorous than
the IMF programme of conditionalities. Thus was born the brutal
Structural Adjustment Programme which featured an exchange rate-
led economic recovery strategy in which the massive devaluation of
the Naira went side by side with the privatisation and commercialisa-
tion of public enterprises, the liberalisation of trade, the removal of
subsidies on social services and petroleum products, the elimination
of price controls, the 'rationalisation' of the country's tariff structure,
the reduction of public expenditure and the deregulation of interest
rates. In seeking to enforce this programme, the Babangida government

> made efforts to weaken and destroy the organised power of
> the popular and other social forces opposed to market reforms
> – forces that are central to the vibrancy of civil society and the
> struggle for democracy. In fact, structural adjustment entailed
> an assault on all social classes in Nigeria.[50]

Nor did the Structural Adjustment Programme deliver. Five years into
its implementation, the 1991 World Bank Report ranked Nigeria as the
13th poorest country globally.

---

[49]*Ibid.* p. 81.

[50] Adebayo Olukoshi,.*op. cit.* p. 385.

After implementing these unpopular market reforms, the Babangida administration became a mirror image of the Buhari regime it had replaced, as it became increasingly contemptuous of human rights and the rule of law. The National Association of Nigerian Students was proscribed, and several journalists were detained. At one point, the Nigerian Labour Congress was dissolved by the regime. Some prominent bankers were dismissed from their jobs while secret groups were formed to break strikes, intimidate students and workers, divide their ranks, and harass social critics. The Babangida regime had announced a detailed political programme of transition to democratic civilian rule in July 1987. Critical to the transition programme was constitution-making. Thus, the government established in September 1987 a forty-six member Constitution Review Committee (CRC) to review the 1979 Constitution; the report of the Political Bureau; and the government White Paper on the report. In February 1988, the report of the CRC was submitted to the government, which then (in April 1988) established a Constituent Assembly with powers to deliberate on the draft constitution and make recommendations to the government.[51] *The Guardian,* one of the country's leading newspapers, criticised the Constituent Assembly's lowly position in the political transition structure thus: 'The transition programme which marginalises the Constituent Assembly and popular participation into a third place in a four-tier constitution process...can be considered flawed *ab initio*.'[52]

Even so, debates in the Constituent Assembly turned out to be a proxy for the continuing discussion about an appropriate federal structure for the country which the Political Bureau had started. Three issues generated heated controversy: Sharia, the status of Abuja and the use of indigenous languages in schools. Some Constituent Assembly members wanted Sharia courts to be expunged from the constitution. Northern members resisted this move and even insisted that Sharia be extended to the Supreme Court. The government intervened and ended the debate on the issue, arguing that 'there already exists a wide measure of national consensus'. There was also controversy over the wording of the Constitution, which stated that 'the provisions of

[51] Rafiu A. Akindele, 'The Constituent Assembly And The 1989 Constitution,' in Larry Diamond, Anthony Kirk-Greene And Oyeleye Oyediran, *Transition Without End*, p. 105.

[52] *The Guardian,* 19 May, 1988.

this Constitution shall apply to the Federal Capital Territory as if it were one of the states of the Federation.' Southerners viewed this phrase as suggesting that Abuja would be treated as just another Northern state, thus increasing the number of states in the North to the disadvantage of the South. They wanted it expunged from the constitution. Again, Northerners resisted this move. The 'Abuja' debate was finally decided to treat the city as Nigeria's capital territory and, therefore, not a state. The Constitution Review Committee had recommended that 'government shall promote the learning of the three main languages namely, Hausa, Ibo and Yoruba in all primary and secondary institutions in Nigeria.'[53] Members from the ethnic minority groups in the South and Middle Belt argued that all languages should be promoted in schools in a multi-ethnic country characterised by multilingualism. The Constituent Assembly eventually approved this position. These debates pointed to divisions between the various ethnic groups in the country, divisions that only a proper federal structure could successfully manage.

Meanwhile, General Babangida's political transition programme to civilian rule was proceeding in a convoluted manner. Early in the life of his regime, Babangida had committed his regime to a handover date of 1 October 1990. In pursuit of this, political parties were registered, then dissolved. In their place, two government-created and funded political parties, the Social Democratic Party (a little to the left) and National Republic Convention (a little to the right), came into being. Politicians of the First and Second Republics were banned, and 'new breed' actors were encouraged to take their place. The handover date kept changing. It became clear to discerning political watchers that General Babangida was reluctant to quit the stage. He was nicknamed 'Maradona' after the Argentinian football prodigy because of his penchant for 'dribbling' the country's political actors. In November 1991, most civil associations in the vanguard of the struggle for democratisation formed an umbrella association that they named Campaign for Democracy (CD). According to Adebayo Olukoshi,

> the chief objective of the CD was to serve as a national pro-democracy coalition, which its members believed had become necessary in view of the reluctance of Gen. Ibrahim Babangida

---

[53] Rafiu A. Akindele, *op. cit..* p. 116.

to complete the transition to civil rule and hand over power to an elected civilian president.[54]

Two news magazines, The News and Tell, critical of the regime's political excesses, complimented the efforts of CD.

The presidential election was eventually held on 12 June 1993. Moshood Abiola, a multi-millionaire businessman and candidate of the Social Democratic Party, was on the cusp of winning when General Babangida annulled the election results in his characteristic manner. The uproar this generated in the broader society was unprecedented. Students and other pro-democracy activists poured out into the streets of the country's cities and towns in protest. The country was still unsettled when General Ibrahim Babangida quit office on 27 August 1993 and handed over to an 'interim' government headed by Ernest Shonekan, a technocrat.

With Ibrahim Babangida, the effort to consolidate political centralism, beginning with the advent of the Second Republic in 1979 and which promised much to federalists but delivered so little, was completed. Babangida had created new states in 1987 and additional ones in 1991, bringing the total to 30. While he claimed that this was done to achieve 'a more balanced Federation' and bring government closer to the people, these new states' economic viability was not considered. Babangida's 30 states were therefore weak and ineffectual and relied on the centre for monthly handouts, further strengthening the latter's position. Babangida not only concentrated power in the centre, but he also personalised that power. He promised democracy and effective leadership, which, if he had delivered, would have bolstered the cause of Nigeria's much-afflicted federalism. As it turned out, however, the Nigerian political arena was turned into a football with which the general nicknamed Maradona practised his skills of motion without movement while the country decayed politically. It took the emergence of Ken Saro-Wiwa and his fellow travellers in the early 1990s for this parlous state of things to be challenged.

---

[54] Adebayo Olukoshi, *op. cit.*. p. 380.

4
Challenging Centralism, or the Spirit of Ken Saro-Wiwa

General Ibrahim Babangida had instituted an elaborate political transition programme beginning in January 1986. The Political Bureau, the Constitution Review Committee and the Constituent Assembly were vital organs of this process. The regime claimed that these provided open platforms for Nigerians to express their views on what sort of political future they desired. However, the military regime had much clandestine influence on these agencies, making Nigerians adopt a cynical view of the entire transition process. Just when the Constituent Assembly had wrapped up its deliberations on the draft Amendment Constitution drawn up by the Constitution Review Committee, there was a bloody and violent continuation of the federalism debate through the instrumentality of a military coup. Led by Major Gideon Orkar, a Tiv from the Middle Belt, Lt. Col Anthony Nyiam from Cross Rivers States and other elements drawn from the various states in the Niger Delta, the coup represented the response of the Southern and Middle Belt minorities to the politics of centralism and a reaction to the dominance by one section of the country that had become more pronounced during the regimes of General Buhari and General Babangida.

The 22 April 1990 abortive coup differed from preceding coups because it was mounted in the name of a particular part of the country. Further, retired non-commissioned officers and some businessmen, including Great Ogboru, a wealthy young businessman from Delta State, played critical roles in executing the coup – unlike in the past. The coup plotters accused the Babangida regime of blatant corruption, economic mismanagement and dictatorial tendencies. As we have seen, calls for confederation had rocked the last days of the Second Republic and the Buhari regime. Orkar and his followers sought a more drastic solution to this debate while the coup took place. They announced in a radio broadcast their decision on the excision of Sokoto, Bornu, Katsina, Kano and Bauchi states from the Federation. Said Major Orkar in the radio broadcast:

This is not just another coup, but well conceived, planned and executed for the marginalized, oppressed and enslaved people of the Middle Belt and the South, with a view to freeing ourselves and our children yet unborn from eternal slavery and colonization by a clique of the country.'

They stated that although the Northern 'cabal'

contributes very little economically to the wellbeing of Nigeria, they have over the years served and presided over the national wealth derived in the main from the Middle Belt and Southern parts of the country, while the people from these parts...have been completely deprived from benefiting from the resources given to them by God.[55]

Eghosa Osagie analysed the deep roots of the coup thus:

Minority spokesmen, especially those of the groups in the oil-producing areas, believed that the national question could only be resolved with justice through the creation of largely autonomous ethnic states, and a restructuring of the revenue allocation system to reverse the unacceptable situation where those whose areas provided the bulk of national revenue but were politically marginalized and the least developed.[56]

The coup was subsequently crushed by officers loyal to the Babangida regime. More than 100 officers and civilians were tried by a military tribunal headed by General Ike Nwachukwu. Sixty-seven military officers were found guilty of participating in the coup and executed. The coup had far-reaching consequences, however. The portion of the federation account allocated to deal with ecological and other problems in the oil-producing areas was increased from 1.5 per cent to 3 per cent. However, this did not stop the tide of unrest in the Niger Delta. The Babangida regime then established the Oil Minerals Producing Areas Development Commission (OMPADEC) in 1992 to coordinate and execute infrastructural and other development projects in the oil-producing communities of Rivers, Delta, Ondo, Edo, Imo and Akwa Ibom states. As will become apparent, however, OMPADEC was not sufficient either.

---

[55] Eghosa E. Osagie, *op cit.* p. 247.

[56] *Ibid.* p.247

The Babangida regime had hardly settled following the neutralizing Major Orkar and his followers when two broad groups came together to convene a national conference. These were 'The Bureaucrats,' comprising prominent former permanent secretaries and parastatal administrators from the Yakubu Gowon days, and 'The Progressives,' an alliance of activists from the Nigerian Bar Association, Civil Liberties Organisation and the Nigerian Labour Congress, among others. The conference sought to discuss all aspects of Nigerian politics, economy and society, including the political transition programme of the Babangida regime and the effects of more than two decades of military rule in the country. The 'National Question' debate had re-emerged.

General Babangida was opposed to the conference and made it clear that his regime would come down heavily on the organisers if they proceeded with it. As a result, 'The Bureaucrats' pulled out of the planned national conference. But 'The Progressives' announced their intention to convene it from 6-9 September 1990.[57] They called the conference 'An Agenda for Democracy.' Sixty-nine organisations, institutions and professional bodies were invited to participate in the conference, including seventy-five 'eminent persons.' Then the regime made its move. However, heavily-armed soldiers sealed off the conference venue the day before the event and delegates were told to disperse. Undeterred, the conference organisers transformed themselves into the standing National Consultative Forum (NCF), with its secretariat in Lagos. According to Adebayo Olukoshi, 'the NCF pledged itself to the pursuit of economic and social justice, fundamental and peoples' rights, a free judiciary, and multi-party democracy, among others. It also pledged to reconvene the national conference at the earliest opportunity.'[58]

The impression has been created that the Northern part of the country was happy with the country's political structure during the Babangida regime and therefore saw no profit in calling for political restructuring. While elements saw the Shehu Shagari-led NPN government of the Second Republic and the Buhari and Babangida military regimes as a welcome continuation of 'Northern Power', others were worried, like their Southern counterparts, at the increasing con-

---

[57] Adebayo Olukoshi, 'Associational Life,' p. 395.

[58] *Ibid.* p. 395.

centration of power in the centre. In addition, they were concerned by the reduction of the states to unviable political entities, heavily dependent on the central government for monthly handouts.

In 1991, a few months after the Babangida regime had prevented the convening of the Lagos national conference, a group of politicians, intellectuals and technocrats from Northern Nigeria held several meetings in Kaduna and Kano 'to design and propose a new federal structure for Nigeria.'[59] This group included Sule Gaya, a former First Republic minister, Tanko Yakasai, Sunday Awoniyi, Suleiman Kumo, Ibrahim Datti Ahmed, Mahmoud Tukur, Sule Yahaya Hamma and Abdullahi Maikano Gwarzo, and others. They were worried about the direction of General Babangida's transition programme. They felt it was without direction and marked by profound insincerity on the part of the regime. The regime had banned First and Second Republic politicians from participating in the transition programme, but the group thought that what was needed in the country was for experienced politicians and technocrats to offer advice and give direction. Furthermore, they were convinced that a North-South alliance was necessary to craft a new constitutional settlement. The group came up with various constitutional, political and fiscal options with which to negotiate with the other parts of Nigeria to restructure the federation. They invited Anthony Enahoro to Kano, held discussions with him and jointly agreed to pursue a restructuring plan. There was, however, disagreements about details, and Enahoro returned to Lagos to launch an independent initiative.

Even so, it must be remembered that the Sule Gaya group was still influential enough on its own to affect the outcome of the June 12 1993 presidential election when a reluctant Babangida regime eventually held it. The group wanted to see an end to military rule, and General Babangida represented military rule at its worst, as far as they were concerned. Further, key members of the group were favourably disposed towards Moshood Abiola, presidential candidate of the Social Democratic Party. They campaigned for him even though Bashir Tofa, a Kano man, was the presidential candidate for the National Republic Convention. When it was clear that Abiola had won, the elections were

---

[59] See Friends Of Democracy, 'Constitutional Review And The Restructuring Of The Nigerian Federation: Our Position' (Memorandum by Friends of Democracy To the National Assembly Committee On The Review of the 1999 Constitution), September 2020.

annulled. Some Yoruba elements in the National Democratic Convention (NADECO), a Lagos-based pressure group whose goal was to campaign for the release of the election results, turned against the North and claimed that Abiola was being prevented from assuming office as President because he was a Yoruba from the South. The NADECO stance was to deepen the political divide between the two parts of the country and became an obstacle to North-South meetings to continue talks on the country's constitutional future.

Anthony Enahoro, who broke with the Northern group in 1991 and returned to Lagos to launch the Movement for National Reformation, was intimately connected with constitutional and political developments since the early 1950s. Indeed, it was Enahoro who, in 1953, moved the motion in the Federal House of Representatives urging that the country be granted independence from Great Britain. The Northern response to the motion triggered much bad blood between the North and South, leading Northern politicians to threaten to pull out of the federation. Enahoro, an ethnic minority from the Midwest, was a leading member of the Yoruba-dominated Action Group at the time. His second moment in the sun came during the ad hoc constitutional conference convened by Col. Yakubu Gowon, who had just taken power following the July 1966 counter-coup launched by Northern officers. As already stated, three of the four regions opted for confederation initially. Only the Midwest delegation, led by Enahoro, called for a federation with a strong centre. Military rule was still a novelty in the country at the time, and Enahoro felt that the interests of the ethnic minorities would be better protected by a powerful Leviathan in the centre. He stuck to this position throughout the 30-month civil war when he was one of Gowon's powerful and trusted advisers. As the Second Republic dawned in 1979, he parted ways with Obafemi Awolowo, his former political leader during the First Republic. Surprisingly, he pitched camp with the Northern-led National Party of Nigeria. The National Party of Nigeria had promised a big umbrella where the leaders of the various ethnic configurations in the country would find shelter. The party, it later turned out, was merely a vehicle through which its leaders looted the national treasury.

When General Babangida seized power in 1985, Anthony Enahoro had abandoned political centralism and became a passionate federalist. He saw now that the all-powerful central government was not only corrupt and incompetent but also went against the grain of the ethnic and religious diversity of the country. The Movement for National Reformation (MNR), which Enahoro birthed in 1991, called for the restructuring of Nigeria into eight regional or provincial federations based largely on ethno-linguistic principles.[60] MNR proposed federations were South-Eastern; East Central; South Central, South-West; West-Central; Northern; North-Eastern and Central. The former convinced centralist had come full circle. Like his former leader Obafemi Awolowo, he now wanted to see a new Nigeria where the large and geographically contiguous ethnic groups would be constituted into distinct federal units. In contrast, the smaller ones would be grouped together. As we shall see in the concluding chapter, however, ethnic federalism in a country like Nigeria has profound problems.

Saro-Wiwa and the Politics of 'Resource Control'

Ken Saro-Wiwa had been writing, since he was a young man of twenty-six, 'The Ogoni Bill Of Rights,' the powerful document advocating the political and economic autonomy of the Ogoni ethnic group within a restructured Nigerian federation. It was presented to the Babangida regime in 1990. The Ogoni, numbering an estimated 500,000 people, are an ethnic minority group in Rivers State. British colonizers were late in putting down roots amongst the Ogoni clans of Babbe, Ken Khana, Nyo Khana, Tai, Gokana and Eleme. Consequently, their neighbours, such as the Ijaw and the Igbo, had a head-start in acquiring Western education and other social amenities. Indeed, it was not until 1947 that the Ogoni had their separate administrative division in the then Eastern Region.[61] Consequently, the Ogoni were under-represented in the colonial administration and educational structures, as they were in their post-colonial institutions after Nigeria achieved self-rule in 1960. The Ogoni have suffered this disadvantage ever since, and it provides the key to understanding the political psychology of its leaders.

---

[60] See Edwin Madunagu, *Biafra And The National Question*, Abuja: Premium Times Books, 2018, p. 4.

[61] The author wrote a doctoral thesis on the struggle of the Ogoni for self-determination in 2002 which was subsequently published as a monograph. See Ike Okonta, *When Citizens Revolt: Nigerian Elites, Big Oil And The Ogoni Struggle For Self-Determination,* Trenton: Africa World Press, 2003.

Ken Saro-Wiwa and other Ogoni leaders like Edward Kobani were in the early 1960s at the forefront in demanding a separate Rivers State. Saro-Wiwa was overjoyed when Col. Gowon, in a bid to undercut Col. Ojukwu's bid for secession, created the Rivers State and the South-Eastern state out of the Eastern Region in July 1967, leaving the majority Igbo with East Central State. In the new Rivers State, where the Ogoni found themselves, the Ijaw ethnic group constituted a clear majority. Saro-Wiwa escaped from Biafra and travelled to Lagos to join the federal side during the civil war. He served as administrator for Bonny, the strategic oil terminal in the Niger Delta, throughout the war. With the war over and the Federal side victorious, he was appointed a commissioner (provincial minister) in the government of Rivers State. Early in the life of the fledgling state, he resented the domination of the Ijaw in key political and economic organs. Thus, was born 'riverain' and 'upland' politics in Rivers State. The Ogoni, Ikwerre, Etche, Ogba and a few other ethnic groups centred around Port Harcourt, the capital, constituted the upland group while the majority Ijaw was the 'riverain'. Saro-Wiwa joined Ikwerre leaders to demand the creation of Port Harcourt State, but nothing came of that effort.

Oil had been discovered in commercial quantities in Ogoniland by Shell Petroleum Development Company (SPDC) in 1958. The Independence Constitution of 1960 spelt out clearly the principle for sharing revenue derived from each part of the federation: 'There shall be paid by the Federation to each Region a sum equal to fifty percent of (a) the proceeds of any royalty received by the Federation in respect of any minerals in that region; and (b) any mining rents derived by the Federation from within that Region.'[62] But, as explained earlier, General Gowon ignored these provisions and went on to decree the confiscation by the Federal Government of all offshore oil. Lamented Saro-Wiwa: 'This action was to usher in that armed robbery of the Ogoni and other delta minorities which has been the hallmark of Nigerian life from 1970 until this moment.'[63] He also drew attention to the action of Second Republic President, Shehu Shagari, who got Pius Okigbo, an economist, to devise a revenue allocation formula for con-

---

[62] Quoted in Ken Saro-Wiwa, *Genocide In Nigeria: The Ogoni Tragedy*, Port Harcourt: Saros International Publishers, 192, p. 84.

[63] *Ibid.* p.84

sideration of the National Assembly. By the time Okigbo was done, the oil-producing minorities had been apportioned only two per cent of their oil. This, according to Saro-Wiwa, was 'bare-faced, daylight robbery' committed by Nigeria's ethnic majorities. But this was not the end of Ogoni's trials and travails. Shell was producing oil recklessly in the Ogoni territory, polluting farmland and fishing streams. There were incessant gas flares and acid rain.

By 1990 Ken Saro-Wiwa and the Ogoni people had had enough. They took stock of their situation in Nigeria and

> found that for all the wealth of their land, and in spite of the fact that an estimated 100 billion dollars had been taken from the land in thirty-two years of oil mining, they had no schools, no hospitals and no roads. They found that there was intense pressure on their land and that they lived in a poisoned environment in which wildlife etc could not survive.[64]

Saro-Wiwa established the Movement for the Survival of the Ogoni People (MOSOP), a grassroots pressure group and wrote the Ogoni Bill Of Rights and had it endorsed by the kings of the Ogoni clans and other leading men of affairs. The Ogoni Bill of Rights demanded that the Ogoni be granted political autonomy to participate in the affairs of Nigeria as a distinct and separate unit and that this autonomy should guarantee:

> (a) political control of Ogoni affairs by Ogoni people; (b) the right to the control and use of a fair portion of Ogoni economic resources for Ogoni development; (c) adequate and direct representation as of right in all Nigerian national institutions; (d) the use and development of Ogoni languages in Ogoni territory; (e) the full development of Ogoni culture; (f) the right to religious freedom; (g) the right to protect the Ogoni environment and ecology from further degradation.[65]

Specifically, the Ogoni Bill of Rights wanted a return to the Independence Constitution revenue allocation formula wherein 50 percent of oil mining revenue was returned to the region from which it was derived.

---

[64] *Ibid*, p.92.

[65] See Movement for The Survival Of Ogoni People, *Ogoni Bill Of Rights*, Port Harcourt: Saros International Publishers, 1990.

General Babangida not only ignored the Bill but proceeded to split the country into 30 states and 589 local government areas, which further marginalized the Ogoni people. The Orkar coup, and the fact that it was led by officers from the oil-producing ethnic minorities, did not go unnoticed by the regime. One other factor forced the regime's hand. The people of Umuechem, an oil-producing community near Port Harcourt, had had, like the Ogoni, enough of Shell, which was extracting oil from their land but gave them nothing in return. So they expelled Shell workers from the Umuechem oil field in July 1990, just as Ken Saro-Wiwa and other Ogoni leaders were about to present the Ogoni Bill of Rights to the Babangida government. Shell called in Nigerian soldiers and anti-riot police. The latter went to Umuechem, killed scores of people, and set several houses on fire. The regime saw the Niger Delta was stirring and decided something had to be done. Babangida's response was Decree 23 of 1992, establishing the Oil Minerals Producing Areas Development Commission (OMPADEC), which increased the 1.5 per cent of oil proceeds allocated to the oil-producing communities to 3 per cent and transferred the fund to the new commission to administer. But OMPADEC was another cynical gesture by the regime to maintain control of the oil-producing communities. Its first executive chairman, Albert Horsfall, was a senior operative of the dreaded State Security Service, which took orders directly from General Babangida. Horsfall soon began to loot the money allocated to OMPADEC.[66] Shell saw the agency as another instrument to bribe its critics in the region and sow division amongst them.

Saro-Wiwa saw OMPADEC for the white elephant it was. He mobilised the Ogoni to expel Shell workers from their oil fields in Ogoniland. This act was peacefully and brilliantly executed by MOSOP, which had now developed deep roots among ordinary Ogoni. There were several branches of the Movement representing the chiefs, youths, women, professionals and other aspects of social life in Ogoni. They met regularly, deliberated on key policies, and arrived at decisions democratically. The Movement decided to boycott the June 1993 presidential election, which was done despite some Ogoni politicians' misgivings. This was when the regime began to sponsor military attacks on the Ogoni, passing them off as attacks from neighbouring

[66] Ike Okonta and Oronto Douglass, *Where Vultures Feast: Shell, Human Rights And Oil*, San Francisco: Sierra Club Books, 2001, pp. 32-33

ethnic groups. Many Ogoni women and men lost their lives and property. When General Sani Abacha in November 1993 swept away the interim government established by General Babangida before he handed over power, the new dictator at first pretended that he was a conciliator. In his inaugural address to the nation, General Abacha promised to convene a constitutional conference with 'full constituent powers' in January 1994. This move was designed to calm pro-democracy activists who had been calling for a Sovereign National Conference since the early 1990s. The new regime set up a nineteen-member National Constitutional Conference Commission and then supervised the election of delegates to the constitutional conference despite the call by pro-democracy activists for the exercise to be boycotted. At the meeting, delegates from the oil-producing areas pressed for a new revenue allocation system that emphasized the principle of derivation. The Conference recommended a new method of revenue allocation, placing greater emphasis on derivation.[67] However, the recommendations of the Conference came to nought as the Abacha constitution was never promulgated into law.

While the constitutional conference was going on in the capital, Abuja, Ken Saro-Wiwa, now President of MOSOP, struggled with divisions within the Movement. On one side were his old friend and political associate Edward Kobani, several other Ogoni notables who disagreed with Saro-Wiwa's uncompromising stance against the Nigerian government and Shell and wanted to commence negotiations with those two parties. On the other side was the new MOSOP President, Saro-Wiwa, backed by the overwhelming majority of MOSOP members, particularly the youth, who wanted nothing less than the implementation of the demands spelt out in the Ogoni Bill of Rights. A battle for supremacy ensued between privileged members of the Ogoni elite and the poor and powerless. Ken Saro-Wiwa was a member of the Ogoni privileged elite, but he chose to cast his lot with the poor.

Things came to a head in May 1994 when Edward Kobani and other elites held a meeting in a village of the Gokana clan. A mob stormed the venue and Killed Kobani and three others. Ken Saro-Wiwa had no hand in the murders. He was far away in Port Harcourt when the tragedy occurred. But the Abacha regime and Shell were anxious to rope in Saro-Wiwa and thus neutralize MOSOP which they saw as a

---

67 Eghosa E. Osaghae, *op cit*, p. 288.

potent threat to the continuous exploitation of oil in the Niger Delta. Saro-Wiwa was arrested the next day and taken into detention. Several other MOSOP leaders were also arrested. The regime also set up a special military task force headed by Lt. Col Paul Okuntimo and ordered it to restore 'order' in Ogoniland. Okuntimo went about this task in a bloody manner, aided and abetted by Shell officials who paid him and the men under his command regularly.[68] The soldiers proceeded to murder, maim, rape and pillage in Ogoniland without restraint.

Ken Saro-Wiwa and eight other MOSOP leaders were found guilty of the murder of the four Ogoni chiefs by a regime-appointed tribunal after a judicially-flawed trial. Despite the efforts of President Nelson Mandela and other world leaders to get General Abacha to set them free, Saro-Wiwa and the MOSOP Eight were hanged in Port Harcourt prison on 10 November 1995. Significantly, a military officer was part of the tribunal that found them guilty. Muhammadu Buhari, Nigeria's current President, was a key member of the General Abacha-led military junta that murdered Ken Saro-Wiwa that bloody morning in Port Harcourt. Said a defiant Saro-Wiwa in a written speech a few days before he was hanged:

> 'I predict that the denoument of the riddle of the Niger Delta will soon come. The agenda is being set for this trial. Whether the peaceful ways favoured will prevail depends on what the oppressor decides, what signals it sends out to the waiting public. In my innocence of the false charges I face here, in my utter conviction, I call upon the Ogoni people, the peoples of the Niger Delta, and the oppressed minorities of Nigeria to stand up now and fight fearlessly and peacefully for their rights.'[69]

Oronto Douglas and the Kaiama Declaration

The challenge to political centralism was sharply posed again only three years after Ken Saro-Wiwa and his followers were murdered. This time it was powered by the Ijaw, the largest ethnic group in the

---

[68] Ike Okonta and Oronto Douglas provided evidence of Shell's culpability in Lt. Col. Okuntimo's reign of murder and terror in their book, *Where Vultures Feast: Shell, Human Rights And Oil*, San Francisco: Sierra Club Books, 2001.

[69] See Ike Okonta and Oronto Douglas, *Where Vultures Feast*, p. 209.

oil-producing Niger Delta and whose land and creeks supplied over half of Shell's daily crude oil output. Like the other dictators before him, General Sani Abacha had placed a network of military task forces in Ijaw territory, fearful that the people would follow the Ogoni example and rise against the oil companies. Following the death of General Abacha in June 1998, his successor, General Abdulsalaam Abubakar, ordered the deployment to the Niger Delta of battle-tested troops returning from peace-keeping duty in war-torn Sierra Leone. Ijaw youth were fully aware of the military build-up and the ring of steel put in place to encircle the Niger Delta. Led by Oronto Douglas, one of the young lawyers who had defended Saro-Wiwa at his tribunal, over five thousand Ijaw youths, drawn from the communities and clans that made up the Ijaw nation, established the Ijaw Youth Council (IYC) on 11 December 1998 and adopted the now historic Kaiama Declaration.

The Kaiama Declaration, like the Ogoni Bill of Rights before it, charged that the quality of life was deteriorating in Ijaw land as a result of utter neglect, suppression, and marginalization visited on the Ijaw nation by the Nigerian state and the western oil companies; that the political crisis in Nigeria was mainly about the struggle for the control of the oil wealth of the peoples of the Niger Delta; and that the unrelenting damage done 'to our fragile natural environment and to the health of our people is due in the main to uncontrolled exploration and exploitation of crude oil and natural gas.'[70] They asserted that all land and natural resources within Ijaw territory belonged to the Ijaw communities and constituted the basis of their survival. The youths declared that the IYC refused to recognize 'all undemocratic decrees that rob our people/communities of the right to ownership and control of our lives and resources, which were enacted without our participation and consent.' Furthermore, IYC demanded an immediate withdrawal from Ijawland of all 'military forces of occupation'. They charged that any oil company that employed the services of the Nigerian armed forces to protect its operations would be viewed as an enemy of the Ijaw people. It also stated that Ijaw youths would take steps to implement these resolutions beginning 30 December 1998. Meanwhile, all oil companies should stop producing oil in Ijaw territory 'pending the resolution of the issue of resource ownership and control in the Ijaw territory.'

---

[70] Ijaw Council of Human Rights, *The Kaiama Declaration*, Port Harcourt, December 1998.

On 28 December 1998, IYC unfolded plans for 'Operation Climate Change,' a series of activities to be carried out between 1-10 January 1999, designed to raise environmental awareness amongst the Ijaw nation. The events were to culminate in non-violent direct action to extinguish the oil companies' gas flares polluting the Ijaw environment. On the morning of 30 December 1998, the ever of the day marked in the Kaiama Declaration as the commencement of activities to implement its resolutions, thousands of young women and men across the Ijaw nation trooped out to the streets and village squares to sing and dance and voice their grievances. They were unarmed. They were not violent. Nevertheless, they were met with a barrage of gunfire from the soldiers deployed by General Abubakar. These troops fanned out into Ijaw towns and villages for several weeks, killing and pillaging. Finally, Lt. Col. Paul Obi, the military administrator of Bayelsa State, declared a state of emergency, the first of its kind since the civil war ended thirty years before. A dusk-to-dawn curfew was also imposed.

Significantly, General Abubakar had ordered the bloody suppression of youths who were asking for a return to federalism and a more equitable share of the resources taken from their land while at the same time overseeing a hurriedly arranged political transition programme for the return to a democratically-elected civilian government. Even as Ijaw youths buried their dead, the presidential elections were being held in February 1999. General Abubakar did not set up a committee to draft a new constitution – or at least Nigerians were not told that he had done so. A Constituent Assembly was not announced. It was only after General Olusegun Obasanjo had emerged as President on the platform of the Peoples Democratic Party that a new constitution was unfurled. The constitution gave enormous powers to the centre and conceded 13 per cent of onshore oil to the oil-producing communities of the Niger Delta. The fundamental principle of consulting citizens and letting them participate in drafting the constitution was observed only in its breach. Thus, Nigeria's Fourth Republic began life in May 1999, resting on a hiatus. The restless spirit of Ken Saro-Wiwa demanding federalism is still abroad.

5
Conclusion:
Bringing Back Federalism

Anti-police brutality protests rocked the country in October 2020. Powered by angry and disenchanted Nigerian youth, the mobilisations had two key moments.

The first was the peaceful demonstrations in key cities in the Southern part of the country demanding the disbandment of the notorious Nigerian Police Force's Special Anti-Robbery Squad (SARS). The youths had accused SARS of extorting, harassing and killing innocent people, especially young men and women. This part of the protest was well organised. The young protestors were peaceful and courteous but determined to have their complaints heard. A few days later, the government announced the disbandment of SARS and its replacement with a new and better-behaved squad. The government also caved into the youths' demand that judicial panels of inquiry be set up in all the states of the Federation to investigate atrocities committed by SARS officers, punish those found guilty and compensate their victims. Even so, the protests did not end. The Lagos suburb of Lekki was the heart of the protests. Youths took over a highway toll plaza in the area. They turned it into a platform where people trooped in to air their grievances against the government of President Muhammadu Buhari.

Three weeks into the continuing protests, when the still enraged youths were about to widen their grievances to include bad governance in the country, the government deployed armed soldiers onto the streets. The soldiers stormed the Lekki Toll Plaza on 20 October 2020, firing live ammunition into the crowd of unarmed protestors who were waving copies of the Nigerian flag in the air and singing the National Anthem. Several young people were killed. The exact number is still in dispute. The following morning, Army Headquarters denied sending armed soldiers to Lekki. Once put on the spot, they changed their stance and said the soldiers dispatched to the toll plaza fired only blank bullets.

The next day the second moment of the anti-police brutality protests kicked in. This time it was led by angry, poor and unemployed youth. In their thousands, they spread out into the towns and cities North and South of the country, forcing open government food stores and helping themselves to their contents. In Lagos, Ibadan and Calabar, the homes and offices of some prominent politicians were targeted and set on fire. The palace of the King of Lagos was also vandalised.

This second part of the protests showed that hunger and anger were ubiquitous in the country. Moreover, the constitutional settlement put in place by General Abdulsalaam Abubakar in May 1999, before he handed power over to democratically-elected President Olusegun Obasanjo, had not delivered prosperity and political stability. Therefore, there was an urgent need for Nigerian citizens to return to the drawing board and craft a constitution that would reflect the social and political diversities of the country.

Twenty-one years after the military quit the stage, the longest period of democratic civilian government in the country's turbulent political history, it might appear that the unitary constitution imposed by General Abubakar was working. But the facts tell a different story. In 2019, the Washington DC-based think-tank, the Brookings Institute, declared Nigeria the world's poverty capital. In December 2020, a World Bank report described the Nigerian economy as being on the brink of 'unraveling'. The international lender singled out the country as being 'uniquely vulnerable' because of its precarious pre-pandemic rising unemployment and inflation, alongside falling incomes and its dependency on oil and remittances. A 9 September 2020 editorial by ThisDay, a daily newspaper, painted a more graphic picture: 'The economy is in tatters, woefully mismanaged as Nigerians get angrier by the day. Millions of people are poorer today than five years ago when the government assumed office. The unemployment rate, officially put at 27 per cent, is probably nearer 50 percent. More than half of the country's young population have no jobs.'[71]

It should be apparent to the discerning that the 1999 Constitution was put in place to facilitate the sharing of oil rent between the central government and the thirty-six states of the Federation, not to encourage self-reliance, creativity and productivity on the part of the latter. Some suggest that the present unitary constitution gives enormous powers to the centre as well as many benefits to the North,

---

[71] *ThisDay*, Lagos, 9 September, 2020.

which is why some Northern politicians and thought-leaders are resisting a more balanced federal constitution that gives increased power to the states and enhancing the derivation principle as obtained in the Independence Constitution of 1960.

The reality, however, is that the present constitution serves no part of the country. All are disadvantaged. Poverty, unemployment, banditry, kidnapping, and general social unrest are pervasive countrywide, even more so in the North than in other parts. As Yakubu Mohammed, the newspaper columnist, wrote in an article in September 2020: 'Home to soulless insecurity with Boko Haram and other assorted criminals, armed bandits, kidnappers, cattle rustlers and herdsmen both local and foreign, unhinged, the once united and peaceful north has turned into a hotbed of grotesque abnormality.'[72]

The North is on fire, as is the rest of the country.

Ironically, the country's political leaders have had plenty of opportunities since 1999 to return to a federal constitution and thus put Nigeria on the path of political stability and economic progress. When Olusegun Obasanjo assumed office as the first president of the Fourth Republic in May, his answer to the Ijaw youths' Kaiama Declaration was to establish the Niger Delta Development Commission, a regional development agency modelled on the failed OMPADEC. However, this move did not stop demands for the restructuring of the country into an actual federal state. When President Obasanjo sent out feelers to leading politicians that he was about to convene a constitutional conference Anthony Enahoro embarked on a nationwide tour to consult with regional leaders concerning an appropriate constitution. In 2003 in Abuja, he held meetings with Northern leaders such as Sunday Awoniyi, Adamu Ciroma, Umaru Shinkafi, Suleiman Kumo, Mahmud Waziri, Ango Abdullahi, among others.[73] Enahoro told his audience that he had consulted with the leaders of the three geo-political zones in the South and wanted to learn about the positions of the three zones in the North. The Northern leaders referred him to the Arewa Consultative Forum (ACF), the umbrella socio-cultural organisation for the North founded in 2001. Enahoro met with the leaders of the ACF, but the discussions broke down.

---

[72] Yakubu Mohammed, 'Cry Not For The North,' *The Guardian*, Lagos, 16 September, 2020.

[73] Friends of Democracy, *Constitutional Review And The Restructuring Of The Nigerian Federation: Our Position*, September 2020.

During the constitutional conference, which was convened in 2005, delegates from the oil-producing states of the Niger Delta pressed for a revenue allocation formula that would place more emphasis on the principle of derivation and asked that the13 per cent of onshore oil given to these states be increased to 30 per cent. They were supported by Igbo delegates. Delegates from the other parts of the country resisted the demand, however. There was a stalemate. Even so, President Obasanjo had different designs for the constitutional conference. He was due to leave office at the end of his second term in May 2017, but he began to plan to elongate his stay in defiance of the constitution's provisions. Obasanjo wanted the constitutional conference delegates and members of the National Assembly to rubber-stamp his 'Third Term' agenda. Frustrated in his bid to stay in office, he dissolved the conference. This was how the first attempt to restructure the country in the Fourth Republic was aborted.

Even as the conference delegates dispersed, the tension in the oil-producing communities was nearing the tipping point. Ijaw youths established the Movement For The Emancipation Of The Niger Delta (MEND). This underground militia began to bomb the installations of the oil companies and also kidnap their workers. The Obasanjo government arrested and detained Asari Dokubo, one of MEND's leaders, but this did not stop the unrest in the Niger Delta. Oil production dropped precipitously, leading to a price surge in the international oil market. As Obasanjo stepped down in May 2007 and was replaced by President Musa Yar'Adua, the oil-producing communities had become a no-go area for oil workers. Armed youth militants roamed the creeks. President Yar'Adua issued an ultimatum for the militants to lay down their arms and be granted amnesty, or else he would deploy troops in the entire Delta region. When the militants demurred, helicopter gunships flew into the delta and bombed several Ijaw villages known to harbour the former. Several youths were killed. It was at this point that the militants agreed to surrender their arms. A standing Presidential Amnesty Programme was established, and several thousand militants were enrolled in it, collecting a monthly stipend from the government. The Yar'Adua government also established the Ministry of the Niger Delta to oversee the new amnesty programme and the failing Niger Delta Development Commission appointed by President Obasanjo in 2000.

One would have expected that with this paraphernalia of intervention measures – 13 per cent derivation, Niger Delta Development Commission, Presidential Amnesty Programme and the Ministry of Niger Delta — prosperity would have returned to the oil-producing communities, and a new era of peace and contentment would be the lot of the people. This is not the case, however. Ordinary people are still as poor and deprived as before, lacking basic social amenities such as roads, hospitals and schools. The oil companies continue to produce oil recklessly, polluting farmlands and fishing waters. Moreover, the governors of the Delta states have been unable to account for how they spent the 13 per cent derivation since 1999.[74] A proper federal arrangement with the constituent states generating and keeping a fair portion of their resources, including oil, would have empowered ordinary citizens of these states to demand accountability from their governors, but this is not the case in present-day Nigeria. There, an all-powerful government in the centre decides how much to allocate to the oil-producing states and when this money would be paid. Thus, the governors of the oil-producing states have, since 1999, regarded the 13 per cent derivation as discretionary income to be spent as they please. Their citizens are treated as powerless supplicants to be thrown a few crumbs from time to time.

It is, therefore, no surprise that the demand for a new federal constitution kept growing even as President Yar'Adua took ill and died in 2010. His successor, Vice President Goodluck Jonathan, was an Ijaw from the oil-producing Bayelsa State. Sensitive to the plight of his people and the demand countrywide for a fresh constitutional compact, President Jonathan convened yet another constitutional conference in 2014. But the Jonathan conference was hamstrung from the outset. The delegates were not elected, despite cries from many quarters for this to be so. Members of the National Assembly did not hide their hostility to the conference, making it clear that senators and members of the House of Representatives were the elected representatives of the Nigerian people and that the constitutional conference delegates were an unwelcome intrusion. To make matters worse, the constitutional conference took place at the same time as President Jonathan was campaigning for re-election, so he was considerably distracted. When the conference delegates concluded their deliberations,

---

[74] *The Guardian*, Lagos, 15 November 2020.

President Jonathan did not bother to send the product of their deliberations to the National Assembly as an executive bill to be passed
into law. Thus was aborted the second time in the life of the Fourth
Republic Nigerians' effort to give themselves a more democratic and
meaningful constitution.

President Jonathan subsequently lost the election to Muhammadu
Buhari of the rival All Peoples Congress in 2015, the first time an opposition party was to replace the incumbent in Nigeria's political history. The All Peoples Congress had boldly stated in its election manifesto that it would restructure the country into a more balanced federation, but President Buhari has not hidden his hostility to the idea.
As far as he is concerned, there is nothing wrong with the unitary
constitution that General AbdulSalaam Abubakar had imposed on the
country in 1999.

Many Voices, One Goal

There is now an accepted consensus among thinking Nigerians that
the 1999 constitution will have to give way to a new arrangement re-
flecting the social complexities of the country. Where these various
voices differ is in the details of the agreed restructuring. Chukwuma
Soludo, an economist and former governor of the Central Bank of
Nigeria, is concerned to craft a new constitution that will speak to
Nigeria's post-oil future. Said Soludo, 'the alternative future that we
see is one without oil, and where other exhaustible natural resources
play very little role. The future economy will be driven by people – our
youths and technology.'[75] Soludo wants to create a 'productive progressive' constitution that would ensure participation and ownership
of the Nigerian project by all citizens of the federation. This stable and
more efficient system would promote fairness, equity and justice. Further, there should be devolution of powers according to the principle
of subsidiarity, away from the current system of 'unitary-federalism.'
He also argued that a proper federation has two federating units and
not three. He proposed that the local government system be scrapped
from the constitution, with states free to create as many local government areas as they desire. The Land Use Act of 1978, the Solid

---

[75] Chukwuma Soludo, 'Economic And Institutional Restructuring for The Next Nigeria', Paper
presented In Lagos on the occasion of the 59th anniversary of Nigeria's Independence, 1 October 2019.

Minerals Act, and the various Petroleum and Gas Acts should be abolished and ownership returned to the federating units. Soludo stated: 'A new fiscal responsibility law could constrain governments at all levels to meet their recurrent expenditures out of their internally generated revenues while revenue from natural resources are deployed only for physical and human capital development.'[76]

Friends of Democracy, a group of Northern intellectuals and politicians comprising Bashir Othman Tofa, Usman Bugaje, Jibrin Ibrahim, among others who came together in September 2020 to submit a memorandum to the National Assembly Committee on the Review of the 1999 Constitution, argued that some protagonists of restructuring tended to articulate their positions as if Nigeria had never before been restructured. But, stated the group, 'the fact of the matter however is that Nigeria has been restructuring since 1914 when the British amalgamated the three territories in the Nigeria area, the colony of Lagos and the two Protectorates to the North and South of the Niger.'[77] Therefore, the current demand for restructuring should be seen as the continuation of a long process to give Nigerians a political arrangement they consider suitable to their present needs. Every part of Nigeria had a peculiar challenge that needed to be addressed, but together all parts had more to gain from a united Nigeria. 'Restructuring must, therefore, not be conceived a priori to be for or against any part of Nigeria.'

The group argued for a return to the 1967 12-state structure that sought to correct the uneven distribution of power between the federal and regional governments. They stated that the distortion of the 12-state structure by multiplying states to 19, 21, 30 and 36 was done to appease new minority groups that emerged after state creation, to spread federal largesse more evenly and sometimes 'for selfish reasons.' Argued the Friends of Democracy, 'today Nigeria cannot sustain the 36-state structure due to its over-dependence on oil revenues that would continue to dwindle in the coming years.' It listed several principles for restructuring Nigeria: states must be economically viable and must rely on fiscal resources they generate themselves instead of handouts from the centre; there must be balance in the distribution of power and fiscal resources between the states and the federation to

---

[76] *Ibid.*

[77] Friends of Democracy, op.cit.

address the desire for local resource control and the viability of the federation as a whole; the 12 states shall be re-designated as regions and shall have complete control of their resources while paying appropriate taxes to the Federal Government; the new regions shall have power to create and maintain local governments as they desire; overhaul the Legislative Lists and reassign agriculture, education and health to the Residual List in which states alone would have competence but the Federal Government would share a regulatory role with the states; the Federal Character principle should be retained and strictly and universally observed; the current Senate should be merged with the House of Representatives under a unicameral legislature; policing should be reassigned to the concurrent list.

Attahiru Jega, an academic and former chairman of the Independent National Electoral Commission (INEC), agrees with Soludo and the Friends of Democracy that the 1999 constitution concentrated too much power and resources in the hands of the Federal Government. Powers that were traditionally the preserve of the federating units were handed over either exclusively to the Federal Government or were shared concurrently by the Federal Government and the states. The present revenue allocation formula (Federal Government: 52.68 per cent; States: 26.72 per cent; Local Government Areas: 20.60 per cent) was heavily tilted in favour of the centre. Jega argued for a return to the two-tier system of federal and states with local government areas subsumed under the states. He disagreed with Friends of Democracy's proposal to return to regions, albeit under the 1967 12-state structure. Argued Jega, 'it would be unrealistic, if not impossible, to revert to a regional structure similar to Nigeria's history. The pressures that led to the creation of states would not tolerate collapsing or regrouping those states to regions.' Nigeria,[78] Jega suggested, should have a short federal exclusive and concurrent list, and whatever was not listed should belong to the states' residual powers, on which the federal government would have only broad regulatory roles. The non-viability of some existing states should be addressed by a decrease in revenues accruing to the centre, an increase in the share of federally collected revenues, and increased capacity and competence by the states in collecting taxes and levies in their jurisdiction. A percentage

---

[78] Attahiru M. Jega, Towards Restructuring Of The Nigerian Federal System: Contribution To A Discussion,' November 2017.

increase to oil-producing states could be accommodated up to a maximum of 5 per cent, bringing the total on account of the derivation principle to 18 per cent. Further, the sharing formula between the federal and state governments should be reviewed in favour of the states, with the latter taking 60 per cent and the former 40 per cent. Argued Jega, 'By working hard and rationally and scientifically to remove all the distortions in our federal system we would have a better functioning federation.'

In his book, Thoughts On Nigerian Constitution, which he wrote in 1966 following the collapse of the First Republic, Obafemi Awolowo made a passionate case for the division of the then existing four regions into eighteen states based on: ethno-linguistic principle. Ken Saro-Wiwa made a similar case in 1990, proposing that the Ogoni should be given a measure of economic and political autonomy as a distinct ethnic group in the Nigerian federation. Anthony Enahoro also followed Awolowo's example, arguing for eight regions to be created based on the ethnic principle. However, Edwin Madunagu, the Marxist and newspaper columnist, strongly opposed using the ethnic principle to restructure Nigeria. Wrote Madunagu,

> It is too late in our history to think of restructuring Nigeria along ethnic lines. Even if this was possible 50 years ago, it is impossible today. Decades of integration has made this impossible. In other words, Nigeria is not the sum of its ethnic groups and I doubt if it was ever so.[79]

While accepting that oppression and exploitation in Nigeria had strong ethnic dimensions, he stated that ethnic separation would not resolve the problem of oppression and exploitation because these evils would be reproduced in newly created states. The Marxist argued:

> Let fighters against ethnic oppression make a distinction, as Rosa Luxemburg did at the turn of the last century, between the right to be free from ethnic oppression and the right to ethnic determination (which historically has included the right to secession). In the Nigerian context the former is a popular-democratic aspiration; it is legitimate; it is correct and it can and will be realised. The latter is unrealisable, even through war.

---

[79] Edwin Madunagu, *Biafra And The National Question*, p. 6.

These are not discordant voices; there are differences in matters of detail, but perceptive thought leaders North and South of the country are united on the fundamentals: the 1999 constitution has proved a disaster. It favours the centre to the detriment of the federating units. The time has come to discard it and craft a new constitutional settlement that will speak to the deep yearnings of Nigerian citizens.

Achieving the New Federal Republic

Ben Nwabueze has written regarding the process of making a constitution: 'A constitution is the act of the people if it is made by them either directly in a referendum or through a convention or constituent assembly popularly elected for the purpose.'[80] The various constitutional conferences in the 1950s and the process of making the 1979 Constitution observed this rule. However, the various constitution-making conferences embarked by the armed forces after 1979 were riddled with blatant interference and a cynical desire by military strongmen to impose a command-style constitutional compact on Nigerians. Even the 1979 Constitution imported the unitary 1978 Land Use Decree and the 1969 Petroleum Decree into the document without a debate by the Constituent Assembly. The nearest Nigerians came to giving themselves a proper constitution after 1979 was the Goodluck Jonathan Constitutional Conference of 2014, but even this was stymied by the lack of appropriate legislation backing the process and giving it sovereign powers.

The time has come to convene a conference with sovereign powers to design a federal constitution for the country. The current process of amending the 1999 Constitution by the National Assembly will not suffice. The document is so hopelessly flawed that only its discarding and a fresh effort at constitution-making will suffice. Some argue that you cannot have two legislative bodies simultaneously, that the National Assembly is the duly-recognised law-making body in the country. However, the truth of the matter is that this is an emergency. Therefore, the National Assembly will have to be prorogued while a popularly-elected constituent assembly deliberates on a new constitution for the country and will re-convene thereafter. The following process is suggested: a popularly-elected sovereign Constituent As-

---

[80] Ben O. Nwabueze, *The Presidential Constitution Of Nigeria*, London: Hurst, 1982, p. 12.

sembly will appoint a constitution-drafting committee, debate the resulting constitution and subsequently present it to Nigerians in a referendum. During the free and open debate in the constituent assembly, various opposing views regarding the details of a federal constitution will be aired and reconciled.

A strong consensus has emerged over time on the federalist content of the new constitution. Like Chukwumah Soludo, Attahiru Jega and Friends of Democracy, I argue for a return to two federating units – the centre and the states. Local government areas should be under the control of the states. I disagree with Friends of Democracy's suggestion that the country be returned to the 1967 12-state structure. While it is true that the various state-creation exercises culminating in the present 36-state structure were the handiwork of unelected military dictators, politicians, and other thought-leaders from various parts of the country, who strenuously lobbied for the creation of these states and indeed heartily welcomed them when they became a reality. There will be loud opposition if an attempt is made to merge some of these states, even as I acknowledge that most of them are presently financially unviable. They can be made to be viable, however. A drastic reduction in the size of the public service and encouragement of agriculture, manufacturing and sundry services will see these states return to viability. The assumption underlying Friends of Democracy's argument for a 12-state structure is that size makes for economic viability. This is not so. Singapore is a small city-state, but it is one of the key financial players in south-east Asia. What really counts is the extent to which all the factors of production in a region or country are galvanised to contribute maximally to the commonweal. Consequently, like Attahiru Jega, I argue for the retention of the present 36-state structure.

Obafemi Awolowo and Anthony Enahoro did not produce convincing arguments for the merging of some ethnic groups into a single state while large ethnic groups like the Igbo, Hausa-Fulani and the Yoruba are allowed to be single states. What is good for the goose should also apply to the gander. Going by Awolowo's ethno-linguistic principle of federalism, then even the smallest ethnic group in Nigeria should be constituted into a separate state. This is not feasible. There are over 300 ethnic groups in Nigeria. Are we seriously suggesting that there should be 300 states in Nigeria? Further, the grouping of the large ethnic groups into single states will amount to a return to the much-lamented Independence Constitution wherein the Igbo, Hausa-Fulani, and the Yoruba dominated their various regions and generated so much inter-regional tension that the First Republic collapsed. Openly incentivising the ethnic principle in a multi-ethnic country has a way of creating ethnic hegemons, leading the latter to challenge the authority of the centre sooner or later. The Ogoni and the other minority oil-producing ethnic communities have had a raw deal in Nigeria, but striking out for an Ogoni state or region as Ken Saro-Wiwa did is not the solution. A more feasible arrangement is a multi-ethnic Rivers State in control of a negotiated and fair portion of its natural resources, which is fairly distributed among the state's constituent ethnic groups.

While disagreeing with Saro-Wiwa's ethnic federalism, I support his argument that 50 per cent of the revenue derived from natural resources should be retained by the region where this resource is produced. Attahiru Jega has suggested that the present 13 per cent of on-shore oil revenue being ceded to the oil-producing states be raised to 18 per cent. This does not go far enough. Indeed, like Chukwumah Soludo, I suggest that the 1969 Petroleum Decree and the 1979 Land Use Act be repealed, and oil and gas returned to the various states that rightfully own them. They should then pay taxes to the central government, up to 50 per cent of this resource. The 50 per cent ceded will be divided into two portions – 20 per cent to the Federal Government and 30 per cent to a pool that will be distributed to the 36 states. I also argue that the principle of derivation should be embedded in the proposed federal constitution to apply to all states in the federation. This will galvanise all the states to look inward to see what wealth can be tapped. This will lead to an increase in the quantum of internally generated revenue. The current practice whereby states depend on monthly allocations from the Federal Government should be repealed immediately. Further, bringing back the principle of derivation will reduce the country's dependence on oil, thereby accelerating the onset of the desired post-oil economy, a new economy powered by manufacturing, agriculture and the intellectual resources of ordinary Nigerians.

There is the argument that the suggested arrangement will benefit the oil-producing states to the disadvantage of the non-producing ones. For one, only four states – Bayelsa, Delta, Rivers and Akwa Ibom are major oil states. The other states in the Niger Delta are marginal producers. While it is true that these four states will see a substantial increase in their revenue, this will be in the short term, however. The industrialised countries of the northern hemisphere are transiting to a post-oil era, and it has been estimated that electric cars and solar energy will replace oil and diesel-powered machines in the next ten years. Following the 2015 Paris Climate Accord these countries are anxious to reverse the harmful effects of climate change, and oil is seen as the primary cause of this condition. To put it bluntly, the oil-producing states in Nigeria and the country have the next ten years to transition to an economy powered by other resources besides oil, or they will be caught in the lurch. The ultimate test of a principle such as derivation is not how it benefits a particular section of the country in the short term but how it benefits the entire country in the long term.

Beyond the arguments and suggestions advanced above, I suggest four broad principles that should animate the proposed constitution. These are civil liberties, democracy, federalism and the Welfare State. Today, the world is replete with illiberal democracies from Poland to Hungary to Russia. Sit-tight dictators conduct elections in Africa and routinely 'win' them. Freedom of speech, the right to peacefully assemble and form political parties and petition the government and the right to a fair trial are under siege. Coming home to Nigeria, the brutal disruption of the anti-police brutality protests in October 2020 brought home the fact that despite enjoying twenty years of uninterrupted democratic rule, Nigerians do not enjoy unfettered civil liberties. Ibrahim El-Zakzaky, the Muslim cleric, has been clamped in detention without trial since 2015 for no other crime. He espouses a denomination of Islam different from the mainstream in Northern Nigeria. Nnamdi Kanu, leader of the Indigenous People of Biafra, was imprisoned and then hounded out of the country because he called for the peaceful secession of the Igbo from Nigeria. Col. Sambo Dasuki, the former National Security Adviser, was accused of embezzling public funds and clamped in detention for several years even as he was undergoing trial. Omoyele Sowore was detained for calling on Nigerians to rise against the manifest failures of the government. This abridgement of civil liberties occurred during the present government of President Muhammadu Buhari. The proposed constitution should rest on a robust platform of civil liberties, making it difficult if not impossible for elected leaders to ride roughshod on the freedoms of citizens.

Federalism thrives best where the institutions of democracy are strong and unfettered. This is because the practice of federalism itself is characterised by debate, negotiation and a general atmosphere of political freedom. Where there is a dictatorship, then federalism is imperilled or killed off altogether. This was what happened during Nigeria's First Republic. The ruling Northern Peoples Congress government's decision to impose a state of emergency on the Western Region when there was no genuine reason to do so was a slide towards dictatorship. When Prime Minister Tafawa Balewa aided Premier Samuel Akintola to rig the 1965 regional election in the same region, he completed the circle of dictatorship. The subsequent killing off of federalism by General Ironsi and his military successors merely followed the path already paved by Balewa's undemocratic actions.

There is one other reason why democracy matters to the practice of federalism. Nigeria has been enjoying an uninterrupted democratic government since 1999, but it is a democracy without development. Indeed, it is a democracy of the ruling class, by the ruling class, and for the sole benefit of the ruling class. The overwhelming majority of Nigerians have not derived any tangible benefits from the practice of democracy. Consequently, there has been a drastic reduction in the number of citizens coming out to vote in recent elections.[81] Ordinary Nigerians do not see any sense in turning out to elect politicians who will look after their personal interests to the detriment of the general populace. Democracy begins to die when people stop voting; and when democracy dies, federalism which rests on it dies too. What is at issue is the limited definition of democracy in Nigeria to mean simply voting at elections. This is wrong. Properly understood, democracy is social and all-encompassing in nature, with the elected and electors alike focused on improving the social and economic conditions of life for all. Where the majority wallow in poverty and neglect even after democracy has been practised for decades, as is the case of present-day Nigeria, then the practice of democracy would have to be radically

[81] *The Guardian,* Lagos, 6 December, 2020.

rethought. It is democracy in this social, inclusive and empowering sense that should be embedded in the proposed constitution.

Federalism has been the default position of the Nigerian constitution since 1950 when the British colonialists first consulted Nigerians as to what constitutional arrangement was suitable for the socially-diverse country. The Founding Fathers negotiated a federal constitution for the country during several constitutional conferences in the 1950s. Successive military governments agreed that a federal compact was the accepted position even as they weakened the institutions underpinning federalism and imposed a unitary system of government on the country. While it is true that the unitary system has its ardent supporters, this system has been tested in Nigeria and has been found wanting. The current practice whereby the 36 states of the Federation troop down to Abuja at the end of every month for handouts and where the centre is saddled with tasks that the states can best execute is the unitary system at its worst. The deafening cries all over the country for this practice to be discarded and a robust federal structure put in its place is a clear and unequivocal vote for federalism. Such positions as those of the Arewa Consultative Forum and President Muhammadu Buhari, who insist that the present unitary constitution is the best system possible for Nigeria, are increasingly in the minority. Federalism should therefore be embedded in the proposed constitution.

A constitution is nothing if it does not provide a clear social and economic framework – an ideological prism – to guide the workers of that constitution. Of all the prominent political actors in Nigeria's First, Second and Fourth Republics, only Aminu Kano spelt out the antagonistic relationship between the haves and the have-nots and the urgent necessity of instituting a government where the needs of the have-nots will be met. The Northern Elements Progressive Union (NEPU) and the Peoples Redemption Party (PRP), the two political parties Aminu Kano established during the First and Second Republics respectively, sought to practice this laudable ideological position. Significantly, the PRP government of Balarabe Musa, which began to implement pro-poor policies in Kaduna State during the Second Republic, was killed off by the rich and powerful only after two years. General Ibrahim Babangida further elaborated this anti-poor stance when he imposed the IMF-inspired Structural Adjustment

Programme on the country in 1986. As a result, public corporations were sold off to the rich, millions of workers were retrenched, and subsidies were removed on such social essentials as healthcare and education. IMF officials assured Nigerians that these measures would eventually lead to economic prosperity. Structural Adjustment has proved an unmitigated failure, however, even as the present government of President Buhari has re-embraced the IMF and its anti-poor policies. The proposed constitution should make the Welfare State practised in Sweden and other Scandinavian countries the cornerstone. There should be universal health coverage free at the point of use, free and compulsory education at primary and secondary levels, generous bursary at higher levels, social housing, unemployment allowance, and robust trade unions. The point of a good constitution is that it lays out a vision of how the welfare of the citizenry can best be secured. The Welfare State, I argue, is the best way to secure the future happiness of Nigerians, particularly the country's poor and powerless.

The proposed constitution should rest on the four broad principles: civil liberties, democracy, federalism, and the Welfare State.

Acknowledgements

I thank Iruka for valiantly and selflessly taking care of the home front in this season of pandemic while at the same time holding down a full-time job of her own. I couldn't have written this little book without her understanding and co-operation.

I thank Innocent Chukwuma, West Africa Representative of the Ford Foundation, who saw merit in the proposal I sent to him and promptly provided the grant that made the research and writing possible.

I thank Dabesaki Mac-Ikemenjima of the West Africa office of Ford Foundation for expertly seeing through the grant process.

I thank Chido Onumah for supervising the research grant efficiently and professionally. At a crucial point in the grant process, Chido's intervention made this book possible.

I thank my brother Ngozi, the usual solid rock of support.

I thank Chiedu Ezeana, with whom I shared several of the arguments subsequently advanced in this book.

I thank Tony Marijy Odidadi and the other members of Saint Patrick's College Asaba Old Boys Association Class of 1979 for providing a convivial social atmosphere that made writing this book a joy.

I thank Chika. The argument is all about her and her generation.

I relied on several people who have thought deeply about the Nigerian crisis in writing this book. Their work considerably lightened the task of writing, but if there are errors of fact or interpretation in this book, I alone bear responsibility.

www.ingramcontent.com/pod-product-compliance
Lightning Source LLC
Chambersburg PA
CBHW070814280326
41934CB00012B/3188